Good Mood, Good Life

Commit to your Self-Love with Care and Good Intentions

Abijah MANGA

MIB Consulting LLC

Copyright © 2022 Abijah MANGA All rights reserved.

The characters and events portrayed in this book are fictitious. Any similarity to real persons, living or dead, is coincidental and not intended by the author.

No part of this book may be reproduced, or stored in a retrieval system, or transmitted in any form or by any means, electronic, mechanical, photocopying, recording, or otherwise, without express written permission of the publisher.

First Edition.

Cover design by: Derek Creative

MIB Consulting LLC Control Number: 20221856975309
www.mabij.net / fondationmabij.com / lovinghomecare.net

Printed in the United States of America

Mabij Consulting LLC
22 Bissette Drive, Colchester VT 05446
(802) 829-0338
info@mabij.net

To my wife Blandine, for her support and insights,

and

my children Elikya, Kimya, Precieux, Mia, David, Deborah, and Gift, without whom this book would not have been written

Contents

Introduction 2

Chapter 1: The Self-Love Formula 5
   What is Self-Love? 5
   How To Cultivate Self-Love 6
   How And why to Practice Self Love 11
   Practice Self-Love and Be Good to Yourself 12
   Learn To Love Yourself 12
   How To Love Yourself for Real 19
   Stick To Facts to Challenge Negative Mental Narratives 21
   Practice Setting Boundaries 24

Chapter 2: Self-Love and Other People 26
   Acquire Life Satisfaction 29
   Develop Healthy Self-Esteem 29
   Develop A Healthy Lifestyle 29
      Focus On Being Someone Who Loves 31
      Stop Comparing Yourself 31
      Ask Your Guidance System for Help 32
      Make Room for Healthy Habits 33
      Postpone Your Worry and Negative Thoughts 33
      Accept What You Cannot Love 34
      Nourish Yourself 35
      Take Yourself Out on A Date 35
      Start A Gratitude Journal 36
      Make Your Body Happy 36

Express Yourself 37
Write A Loving Letter to Yourself 37
Shower Yourself in Feel-Good Vibes 38
Steps To Practice Self Love Everyday 40
Recognizing And Accepting Your Emotional State 40
Take Time for Yourself 41
Get Enough Sleep 42
Exercising 42
Eating Right 43
Using Self-Talk 44
Challenging A Negative Story About Yourself 45
Forgiving Yourself 45
Committing To Self-Love 46
Commit To Learning More 46

Chapter3: Reconnecting with Your Body 48
What Is Disconnection Like? 50
What Causes Disconnection? 51
Non-Judgment 54
Bring It All Together 54
The Struggle to Stay Connected 56
Stress And Pressure 57
Societal Expectations and Judgement 57
Personality And Passion 58
Building Your Body Intelligence 58
Responding with Self-Compassion 59
Some Ways to Reconnect with Your Body 61
Do Yoga 61
Jump in a Cold Shower 62

Sing..62
Grab a Snack..62
Hold Your Breath..63
Walk Barefoot..63
Dance N' Groove..63
Run for the Hills...64
Get a Massage...64

Chapter 4: Positive Self-Talk...65
The Connection between Mental and Physical Health............67
Implementing Positive Self-Talk in Your Daily Routine..........68
    Ensure The Positive Self-Talk Feels True..............................68
    Change Your Behavior..68
    Start With Positive Self-Talk in One Area............................69
    Collect All the Data Without Judgment................................69
    Question Your Thoughts...70
    Work With a Professional...70
What are the Benefits of Positive Self-Talk?................................71
What Impact Does Negative Self-Talk Have?............................72
The Power of Positive Self-Talk...73

Chapter 5: Meditation for Self-Love...77
Stepping into Self-Love..78
Meditation for deep self-and-other-healing................................83

Chapter 6: The Importance of Self-Love.................................92
The Ills of Perfectionism..93
Moving Away from Perfectionism...94
What is Self-Compassion?...94
Tips And Techniques for Practicing Self-Compassion.............97

Becoming More Self-Aware 97
Regaining Perspective 99
Developing Self-Compassion 102
What Gets in The Way of Self-Love? 104
Tools to Practice and Strengthen Your Self-Love 106
   To Liberate Yourself from Comparisons 114
   To Live Life in Alignment with Values 115
   Confidence 116
   Resilience Through Challenges 116
   Maintain Healthy Relationships 117

Chapter 7: Self-Awareness 118
What are Self-Awareness Skills? 120
Tips for Becoming More Self-Aware 121
Self-Awareness Takes Courage 124
Taking Care of Yourself is Crucial 125
Contradictions are Normal and Human 125
The Role of Self-Awareness in Therapy 126
How Do You Become More Self-Aware? 127
Importance in Counseling and Coaching 129
Self-Awareness Emergence 130
Self-Awareness Development 131
Self-Consciousness 131

Chapter 8: Self-Exploration 133
Act Authentically 135
Use Self-Affirmations 136
Confront Your Inner Critic 136
Don't Hide Your Imperfections 137

Find Who You Are Not 137

Chapter 9: Self-Care 142
What Are the Barriers to Self-Care? 143
What Types of Self-Care Are There? 144
What Are the Benefits of Self-Care? 145
How to Build a Self-Care Plan 146

Chapter 10: Self-Esteem 155
Why Self-Esteem is Important 156
Replace Negative with Positive Thinking 158
    Use Positive Affirmations Correctly 162
    Identify Your Competencies and Develop Them 163
    Learn to Accept Compliments 163
    Introduce Self-Compassion, Not Self-Criticism 163
    Affirm Your Real Worth 164
Self-Esteem Check 164
Range of Self-Esteem 165
Benefits Of Healthy Self-Esteem 166
Adjust Your Thoughts and Beliefs 168

Conclusion 172

"Thou shalt love the Lord thy God with all thy heart, and with all thy soul, and with all thy mind. This is the first and great commandment. And the second is like unto it, Thou shalt love thy neighbour as thyself"

– (Matthew 22:37–39).

Introduction

There's a lot of discussion about self-love these days. It sounds nice, but what exactly does it mean? How do we love ourselves, and why is it important? Self-love entails accepting yourself, treating yourself with compassion and respect, and nurturing your growth and well-being. Self-love includes how you treat yourself and think and feel about yourself. So, when you think about self-love, consider what you would do for yourself, how you would communicate to yourself, and how you would feel about yourself that expresses love and concern.

When you love yourself, you have a good outlook on yourself. This does not imply that you are always pleased with yourself. That would be impossible! For example, I may be sad, furious, or dissatisfied with myself while loving myself. If this is unclear, consider how this works in other partnerships. I can love my son even when I am upset or unhappy with him. Even in the middle of my rage and disappointment, my love for him shapes how I interact with him. It enables me to forgive him, respect his feelings, address his needs, and make decisions that benefit his health. Self-love is extremely similar.[1]

If you grew up without any role models for self-love or someone telling you how important it is to be kind to yourself, you might dispute its worth. Without self-love, you're more inclined to be self-critical and succumb to people-pleasing and perfectionism. You are

---

[1] "Good Vibes, Good Life: How Self-Love Is the Key to Unlocking Your ...."
https://www.goodreads.com/book/show/42186465-good-vibes-good-life.

more willing to tolerate others' abuse or mistreatment. You may disregard your wants and feelings if you do not value yourself. Furthermore, you may self-sabotage or make judgments, not in your best interests. Self-love is the foundation for being assertive, setting boundaries, creating good relationships with others, practicing self-care, pursuing our interests and objectives, and feeling proud.

Aside from whether self-love is truly important, another major impediment to self-love is the idea that it is narcissistic or selfish. When psychologists and therapists urge self-love, they are not referring to elevating oneself above others. Narcissists feel better than others and refuse to admit or accept responsibility for their shortcomings and failures. They also want further external affirmation and acknowledgment. Narcissists lack empathy for others as well.

On the other hand, self-love isn't about bragging about how wonderful you are. People who healthily love themselves recognize that they are flawed and make errors, but they accept and care for themselves despite their flaws. Self-love does not exclude you from caring about others; it just means that you may treat yourself with the same compassion that you do others.[23]

It's natural to feel conflicted about self-love or making any change. However, loving yourself does not imply that you must modify every aspect of your life. Simply strive to treat yourself better than you did yesterday. First, I recommend that you think of one nice act you can

---

[2] "Self-Love and What It Means - Brain & Behavior Research Foundation." 12 Feb. 2020, https://www.bbrfoundation.org/blog/self-love-and-what-it-means.

[3] "What is Self-Love and Why Is It So Important? - Psych Central." 31 May. 2019, https://psychcentral.com/blog/imperfect/2019/05/what-is-self-love-and-why-is-it-so-important.

do for yourself today. It might be a reassuring idea or deed. Next, write down what you want to accomplish and when you intend to do it. Writing it down promotes accountability and raises the likelihood of you following through. As you incorporate more loving ideas and deeds into your everyday life, some of your self-defeating beliefs and habits will fade away. Self-love will become second nature with practice.

CHAPTER 1

The Self-Love Formula

Today, self-love is a buzzword thrown around casually: "You need to love yourself more." "How come you don't love yourself?" "This would not have happened to you if you had simply loved yourself." "You can't love another person unless you first love yourself." These are just a handful of the self-love commandments we give or get to help us live more fulfilled lives. Self-love is essential for living successfully. It impacts who you choose as a partner, the image you display at work, and how you deal with challenges in your life. It is so vital to your well-being that I want you to understand how to incorporate more of it into your life.

What is Self-Love?

Is self-love something you can get via a beauty makeover or a new outfit? Can you increase your supply by reading something inspirational? Can a new relationship make you fall in love more deeply with yourself? All of these questions are answered in the negative. Self-love is more than just a wonderful sensation. A sense of self-esteem develops due to behaviors that promote our physical, psychological, and spiritual development. Self-love is dynamic; it develops due to behaviors that mature us. Having compassion for ourselves as human beings who are searching for meaning in our lives and acting in ways that foster self-love in ourselves allows us to accept our strengths and flaws more readily, reduces our need to rationalize our shortcomings, and allows us to be more focused on our life's purpose and values and expect to find fulfillment through our efforts.[4]

How To Cultivate Self-Love

- **Be mindful:** People who love themselves are more aware of what they think, feel, and want. They are aware of who they are and act on this understanding rather than what others wish for them.

- **Act on what you require rather than what you desire:** You love yourself when you can turn away from what feels wonderful and exciting and instead focus on what you need to keep strong, grounded, and going ahead in your life. By focusing on what you need, you may avoid the habitual behavior patterns that get you into problems, keep you locked in the past, and reduce your self-esteem.

---

[4] "Self Love: Definition, Tips, Examples, and Exercises." https://www.berkeleywellbeing.com/self-love.html.
"Self-love - Wikipedia." https://en.wikipedia.org/wiki/Self-love.

- **Practice good self-care:** When you take better care of your fundamental needs, you will love yourself more. People who value themselves nurture themselves regularly through healthy activities such as adequate eating, exercise, proper sleep, intimacy, and positive social relationships.[56]
- **Set boundaries:** When you establish limits or say no to job, love, or hobbies that deplete or injure you physically, emotionally, and spiritually, or express poorly who you are, you will love yourself more.
- **Protect yourself:** Bring the appropriate individuals into your life. I adore the phrase frenemies, which I picked up from one of my younger customers. It perfectly depicts "friends" who enjoy your agony and loss rather than your happiness and achievement. My advice to you is to get rid of them! Then, you will have a greater love and regard for yourself.
- **Forgive yourself:** We humans can be quite critical of ourselves. The disadvantage of accepting responsibility for our actions is that we punish ourselves excessively for errors in learning and improving. Before fully loving yourself, you must embrace your humanity (the truth that you are not perfect). When you make a mistake, try to be kinder to yourself. Remember that if you have learned and evolved from your errors, there are no failures, simply lessons learned.
- **Live intentionally:** Regardless of the circumstances of your life, you will be able to accept better and value yourself if

---

[5] "What is Self-Love | The Importance of Self Love | How to Practice Self ...." https://www.growingself.com/what-is-self-love/.
[6] "Self-love - Wikipedia." https://en.wikipedia.org/wiki/Self-love.

you live with a clear sense of direction and purpose. You don't have to know exactly what you want to accomplish. Every time you succeed in reaching your life goals, you will feel better about yourself because you made the right choices to get there in the first place. In addition, you will love yourself more if you see yourself achieving your goals.

You will properly learn to accept and love yourself more if you focus on just one or two of these self-loving behaviors. Consider how much you'll appreciate yourself once you've followed these seven steps to self-love. True, you can only love someone as much as you love yourself. If you practice all of the self-love behaviors I've described here, you will allow and encourage others to do the same. The more you love yourself, the more prepared you are for successful relationships. More importantly, you will begin to attract people and circumstances that promote your well-being.

If you're like most individuals, your answer varies according to the day. Even if your hair is messy, you may feel great and attractive. On the other hand, you focus on a pimple on your chin or the dark bags beneath your eyes on other days. It's normal and even good for your sentiments regarding self-acceptance to fluctuate. One of the most common myths about fiercely loving oneself is that you must adore every aspect of yourself every day. Nobody likes everyone all of the time, and the same goes for how you feel about yourself. True self-acceptance is being open about your feelings and who you are, flaws and all.[7]

---

[7] "Self-Love and What It Means - Brain & Behavior Research Foundation." 12 Feb. 2020, https://www.bbrfoundation.org/blog/self-love-and-what-it-means.

Be compassionate by treating yourself with care, especially through difficult times (since you will need it the most). Be deliberate in your daily selections; our lives are the sum of the succession of choices we make. Finally, be honest about what you enjoy and dislike. What are your strong points and weak points? Only through such candor can you gain enough self-awareness to force change and growth.

We allow ourselves more freedom to grow into the person we want to be if we begin each day acknowledging that we are not perfect but good and enough. The fact that we carry a picture of the person we aspire to be is a testimonial to our character, ambitions, and trust in ourselves to become the same thing that motivates us. "I am learning every day to let the distance between where I am and where I want to go to inspire me rather than fear me," Tracee Ellis Ross says. Next, challenge yourself to work on yourself nonstop. This approach will most likely look extremely different depending on who you ask. However, there are three things that everyone should strive to achieve.

Everything you do, from what you eat for breakfast to how you spend your leisure time, is or may be an investment in yourself. So, shower yourself with excellent and wholesome things that will positively impact your life.

You are skilled in one area. You're not simply good or even exceptional. There is something that you are extremely good at. Don't stop till you figure it out. You must know what it is for yourself, but keep in mind that the rest of the world is waiting for you to

---

"What is Self-Love and Why Is It So Important? - Psych Central." 31 May. 2019, https://psychcentral.com/blog/imperfect/2019/05/what-is-self-love-and-why-is-it-so-important.

discover your talent. Working hard for tomorrow and the future is part of the challenge, as is synchronizing the activities we need to do now to become the person we want to be. But keep in mind that tomorrow is not assured. Nothing in life is. So, enjoy yourself along the way. Take pleasure in the process for what it is. It will not fight you until you fight it.

These three things are only possible if you are caring, insightful, and honest. There are difficult days, just as there are pleasant ones. Don't be scared to take a pause or weep if necessary. That is not a sign of weakness but rather a courageous decision to listen to yourself and respond as needed. It demonstrates that you are adaptable and can deal with anything life throws at you, good or bad. You will need both your physical and mental health to overcome anything in this life. Even if you are lovely, you will not always feel that way. You know that beauty comes from inside, so use such days to urge you ahead. Every day, actively display self-love and be your own best friend.[8,9]

To put it into action, we must first understand what it means. There are many ways to cultivate self-love, but one of the most important is by engaging in activities that help us grow as individuals. To be self-loving, you must place a high value on your enjoyment and well-being. Being self-aware and self-reliant are two of the most important aspects of self-love. To be self-loving, you must refuse to accept anything less than you are capable of. Because we all practice self-care in different ways, "self-love" can imply different things to different individuals. An important part of your mental health is

---

[8] "Self Love: Definition, Tips, Examples, and Exercises." https://www.berkeleywellbeing.com/self-love.html.
[9] "Self-love - Wikipedia." https://en.wikipedia.org/wiki/Self-love.

knowing what self-love is on your terms. Practicing self-love means appreciating yourself for who you are right now. Embracing your feelings and prioritizing your physical, emotional, and mental well-being are key components of this approach to living fully.

How And why to Practice Self Love

To summarize, it is clear that valuing oneself is an important factor in making wise decisions in one's daily activities. It is easier to make choices in your best interests when you place a high value on your self-worth. These things might include eating well, exercising, or having healthy relationships. Among the ways to cultivate self-love are:

- Becoming more aware. People who love themselves are more aware of what they think, feel, and want.
- Taking activities based on need rather than desire. By focusing on what you need, you may avoid the habitual behavior patterns that get you into problems, keep you locked in the past, and reduce your self-esteem.[10]
- Taking care of oneself. When you take better care of your fundamental needs, you will love yourself more. People who value themselves nurture themselves regularly through healthy activities such as adequate eating, exercise, proper sleep, intimacy, and positive social relationships.
- Making a place for good behaviors. Begin caring for yourself by reflecting on what you eat, exercise, and do with your

---

[10] "What is Self-Love | The Importance of Self Love | How to Practice Self ...." https://www.growingself.com/what-is-self-love/.

time. Do things not to "get it done" or "have to," but because you care about yourself.

To practice self-love, begin by treating yourself with the kindness, patience, gentleness, and compassion you would show to someone you care about.[11]

Practice Self-Love and Be Good to Yourself

Loving oneself takes happiness and security to a whole new level. We seek affection openly because that is how we find love and stability as children. It was given to us as a prize for doing good. But we didn't grow out of it; we still look for love in other people, but the fact is that the love you seek can only come from inside. That is why someone else's affection will never be enough to make you genuinely happy, and you will never feel secure if you are not confident in your talents. But how can you become more self-assured and love yourself? We cultivate self-love to overcome limiting ideas and live a genuinely shining life.

Learn To Love Yourself

Please do yourself a favor. Take a deep breath, hug yourself, and begin practicing the following self-love tips:

Perfect physique, vitality, intelligence... Everything. Perfection does not exist, and when it appears on social media, it frequently disguises terrible mental health difficulties. You will never achieve perfection. But the good news is that you are already perfect in your

---

[11] "Self-Love | Psychology Today." 12 Nov. 2019, https://www.psychologytoday.com/us/blog/the-upside-things/201911/self-love.

flaws. Even if you achieve a ludicrous goal, you'll always be disappointed because you'll always want more. It's human nature.

Take a break from the never-ending search and look inside. Consider where you've come from and the beauty of the fact that YOU ARE ALIVE - a living, breathing, functional human being — and how rare it is.

That is the secret to contentment. Begin a thankfulness diary, an Instagram account, a blog, or just spend 3 minutes each day thinking about everything you are grateful for – your body, your life, your friends, your nation, M&Ms, how long that old pan has lasted you, how that person on the bus let you off first... We become resentful when we get comfortable. Change it by expressing thankfulness daily. You do not influence other people, decisions, or conduct, just as you have no power over the weather. [12]

Society has taught us that self-care is selfish, and God forbid, being labeled selfish is our biggest dread. As a result, we labor ourselves to death so that everyone may see how Good we are. But there is a cost to being "Good" in society's eyes, and that cost is your happiness. Stop striving to be "Good" and start taking care of yourself. Self-care equals happiness. Begin by incorporating these 30 Self-Care Habits for a Strong and Healthy Mind, Body, and Spirit. Find a seat, get a coffee, and tell me about your day. What are your thoughts? Feel that sensation. The greatest path ahead is to learn to feel your sensations rather than push them under the rug.

---

[12] "8 Powerful Steps to Self-Love | Psychology Today." 29 Jun. 2017, https://www.psychologytoday.com/us/blog/the-mindful-self-express/201706/8-powerful-steps-self-love.

Ask them whether they are true. Are they beneficial? Are they considerate? Before you say anything bad, consider whether it will help you. Is this notion making me better in any way? Is it merely unpleasant, demeaning, and cruel? We are typically the harshest to ourselves mentally; thus, stopping internal pain is one of the most fundamental steps to happiness. The constant taunts and demeaning, the "you're such this and that." In your brain, just use encouraging and uplifting phrases.

Take a look at who you are due to the five individuals you hang out with. Who exactly are they? Are they upbeat? Loving? Supportive? Or are they pessimistic, unpleasant, and abusive? Therefore, you owe no one anything, whether you have a particularly negative buddy, an insulting partner, or a pretty opinionated bossy Aunt. You owe them nothing but your time. Ditch, avoid, and proceed. Your life is at stake.

Not only that, but if you consume something you deem nasty, you sit and feel horrible about yourself. Don't criticize yourself for consuming food; life is too short of criticizing yourself. Remove the food restrictions, quit dieting, and eat like a person. Consume meals that you enjoy and that are natural. Your body will appreciate it. Don't just join a gym and never go. Try out a new type of physical exercise; pick one that you appreciate, makes you laugh, and enjoy. Then do it! Dancer, Zumba, spin classes, mermaid swimming...

There are virtually infinite sports available. Try them out and watch your happiness grow![13][14]

You've gone through a lot, getting stronger and stronger each time. But I would like you to remember who you are. Adversity is your buddy; it pushes you to make life more fascinating, so you can go where you want to go! Your body is a fantastic and lovely tool for exploration. Your body was not created to be only attractive to impress others and society. It's not a high-end Vase. But it is a tool that allows you to accomplish all of your goals in life. Climbing, eating, traveling, working, knitting... Take care of your body as if it were a child. With nothing but love and the awareness that everything is beautiful just like it is. We are told that we will be happy if we fit into the Ideal Body. You know the kind; it shifts with each decade, an unachievable beauty standard frequently airbrushed over.[15][16][17]

No matter how much weight you lose, how much plastic surgery you have, or how many goods you purchase. Happiness cannot be discovered in a body since happiness does not exist. Self-acceptance leads to happiness. Realize that you desire a body to feel safe,

---

[13] "41 Ways to Practice Self-Love and Be Good to Yourself." 10 Mar. 2022, https://www.lifehack.org/articles/communication/30-ways-practice-self-love-and-good-yourself.html.

[14] "Just Love Yourself: 5 Must-Know Self-Love Techniques." 10 Jan. 2020, https://blog.mindvalley.com/self-love-techniques/.

[15] "What is another word for self-aware? - WordHippo." https://www.wordhippo.com/what-is/another-word-for/self-aware.html.

[16] "10 Simple Ways to Improve Your Self-Awareness [With Examples]." 04 Nov. 2021, https://nickwignall.com/self-awareness/.

[17] "Self-awareness Definition & Meaning - Merriam-Webster." https://www.merriam-webster.com/dictionary/self-awareness.

accepted, and successful, so you can accomplish whatever you want to do.

True pleasure and love are found in appreciating and experiencing what you have. Not that you had a large collection or were a hoarder. Shopping for happiness is like getting a McDonald's lunch, whereas appreciating what you have is a prepared nourishing meal. Here's a book recommendation for you: What can buy happiness if money cannot?

Remove all of the nasty individuals from social media. All of those relatable memes about underachievers. Not everything you think is true. We all have an inner critic attempting to keep us tiny and secure. The disadvantage is that this prevents us from enjoying a complete life.

Surround yourself with individuals who will love and support you. Allow them to remind you of how awesome you are. Take a look at who you are due to the five individuals you hang out with. Who exactly are they? Are they upbeat? Loving? Supportive? Or are they pessimistic, unpleasant, and abusive? Therefore, you owe no one anything, whether you have a particularly negative buddy, an insulting partner, or a pretty opinionated bossy Aunt. You owe them nothing but your time. Ditch, avoid, and proceed. Your life is at stake. Looking for techniques to teach yourself to love yourself? Keep this in mind. Because there is no one else on the earth like you, you cannot reasonably compare yourself to anybody else. You should only compare yourself to yourself.

Get rid of any unhealthy relationships. Seriously. Anyone who makes you feel less than magnificent does not deserve to be in your life. Celebrate your victories, large or little. Be proud of what you've accomplished and pat yourself on the back. This is a wonderful method to love and be pleased with oneself. Trying something new is one of the best ways to appreciate oneself. It's a great feeling to discover you've accomplished something you didn't know you could do before. If you wish to practice self-love, accept and appreciate your differences. This is what distinguishes you. Every day, take some time to relax your thoughts. Breathe in and out, empty your mind of thoughts, and simply be. Do you know that stuff that gets you thrilled but also worries you? You want to accomplish something but have convinced yourself that it would not work. You should go ahead and do it![18][19]

Self-esteem is always changing. It must be done daily yet might take a lifetime to perfect. So be gentle to yourself and support yourself at difficult times. Be aware of your thoughts, feelings, and desires. Live your life in such a manner that it reflects this. That is not to say that everyone will always return the favor, but that is their problem, not yours. Reach out to family, friends, healers, or anybody else who can assist you in getting through the difficult times. You are not supposed to face them alone. Understand how to say no. Saying no occasionally does not make you a terrible person; rather, it makes you wise. You know that thing you did once (or twice) that made you feel horrible, humiliated, or ashamed? It's time to let go of it. You can't undo what you've done in the past, but you can influence your future. Consider it a learning experience, and have faith in your improvement abilities.

---

[18] "The importance of self-love and how to cultivate it." 23 Mar. 2018, https://www.medicalnewstoday.com/articles/321309.
[19] "How to Be More Self Aware: 8 Tips to Boost Self-Awareness." 17 Oct. 2019, https://www.developgoodhabits.com/what-is-self-awareness/.

Is your mind racing with so many ideas that it's giving you a headache? No matter how insane, cruel, sad, or terrible they are, write them all down. Keep it in a notebook, rip it up, burn it, whatever it takes to get rid of it. There will be no TV or other distractions, just you. Consider the good things in your life and your huge aspirations and how you may make them a reality. Do you understand why? We are all human, after all. We make errors and experience emotions (both positive and negative), which is perfectly normal. Allow yourself to be a human being. Get creative and express yourself as you want. Painting, writing, sculpting, constructing, music, anything you want, and leave your inner critic at the door. There are no correct methods of being creative.

This may be a very difficult situation, and you may need to seek assistance from others. However, when we let go of things that have happened to us, it is almost as if a weight is lifted off our shoulders. We no longer have to take that around with us. We are entitled to better. Where is it that you feel completely at peace, calm, cheerful, optimistic, and alive? When you are going through a difficult period, travel to that spot or picture yourself there. Consider how it feels, how it smells, and how it appears. Make a list of your greatest characteristics and accomplishments the next time you feel pleased and on top of the world. It's time to make a change if it's anything less than kind, encouraging, and supporting. You are entitled to be addressed in the same way you would address your closest friend, sister, brother, daughter, or son.[20]

---

[20] "About Self-Love: What is Self Love?." https://pathofselflove.org/about/about-self-love/.

How To Love Yourself for Real

Advice on how to love oneself is everywhere these days. Step into your favorite neighborhood gift store. You'll likely discover rose quartz-topped self-love manifesting candles, positive-affirmation card decks, and pillows embossed with Brene Brown self-compassion phrases.

Self-esteem sells. But do we believe it? Kat from Euphoria isn't, but while it may seem trite or simplistic, most mental health specialists will tell you, in one way, that being nicer to and more accepting of oneself is vital for both mental health and successful relationships. Unfortunately, however, several things (for example, trauma, years of self-criticism, and systematic prejudice) can make this seemingly straightforward practice far more complicated—and far easier said than done. That's why we sought the advice of a few therapists who specialize in the subject. Continue reading for their practical advice on how to (really) love yourself—no inspirational quotes necessary (but no shame if those help you, either).

Consider your closest friends and family members who show up with affection for you even when you are at your worst, least successful, insert-negative-adjective-here self. "When we learn that perfection is not necessary for being loved by other people or enjoying ourselves," Adia Gooden, Ph.D., a licensed clinical psychologist whose TED Talk on "unconditional self-worth" has been seen nearly 1 million times, tells SELF. But anybody who has struggled with would, should, and could understand that accepting your flaws and defects can feel nearly impossible. "When I deal with clients, I realize that most of their pain stems from a desire for things to be different than they are," Goodman says. She employs a dialectical behavior therapy technique known as "radical acceptance" to assist individuals in accepting the realities of their life while also maintaining optimism for the future.

This technique is based on the idea that to embrace our flawed selves, we must first acknowledge our reality. "What we oppose endures," explains Dr. Gooden. In other words, denying what's occurring increases your chances of engaging in negative self-talk. Conversely, if you practice nonjudgmental acknowledgment of your reality ("This is my circumstance" or "This is what happened"), you'll be better equipped to accept and move past the things you can't control. Dr. Gooden emphasizes the term "accept"—you don't have to enjoy what's going on. It's reasonable to be sad that you weren't called back for a second interview, but recognizing the facts of the situation might help you avoid feeling like a letdown. The goal is to avoid falling into a self-blame spiral by first acknowledging your ideas and feelings and then practicing self-acceptance rather than continuously berating yourself for what you should've done differently.

According to Dr. Gooden, another practice that helps build self-love and acceptance is self-forgiveness. Again, forgiveness is frequently easier in principle than in reality, but one approach she suggests absolving yourself is to recognize the learning you acquired from a disheartening experience. If, for example, a relationship fails, try not to be too harsh on yourself for the five months you put in the other person or behavior you're not proud of. Instead, consider what you learned throughout those months that will help you in the future. Dr. Gooden explains that self-love does not exclude us from making errors; rather, it encourages us to accept responsibility when we do something we don't like so that we may move ahead more readily.[21][22]

It's also worth noting that the process of learning to accept and forgive oneself can elicit intense grief. "When you consider how much time you've spent beating yourself up, comparing yourself to others, or convincing yourself that you were awful or damaged," Dr. Solomon adds. Allowing yourself time to grieve is acceptable and even beneficial, she adds, as long as you finally focus on embracing whatever occurred in the past to move forward—and embrace your future as an opportunity to live differently.

Stick To Facts to Challenge Negative Mental Narratives

Buddhists depict suffering as two arrows. The first arrow represents an awful occurrence that occurred to us—a painful arrow that was beyond our control. The second arrow represents the tale we tell ourselves about that event—this is self-inflicted misery. Dr. Solomon defines self-love as avoiding shooting oneself with the second arrow. The first arrow, for example, may represent the death of a loved one from COVID-19. The second arrow may be you convincing yourself that they would not have died if you had persuaded them to go to the doctor sooner. Or it may be you persuading yourself that even though they weren't vaccinated, you should have spent the holidays with them. In other words, while a circumstance might be emotionally terrible, the story we tell

---

[21] "10 Tangible Ways To Practice Self-Love—Lists, Rituals & More." 13 Feb. 2020, https://www.mindbodygreen.com/0-12428/10-wonderful-ways-to-practice-selflove.html.
[22] "Pentingnya Self-Love dan Cara Menerapkannya - Alodokter." https://www.alodokter.com/pentingnya-self-love-dan-cara-menerapkannya.

ourselves about it is frequently the root of our anguish. Dr. Solomon adds, "The good news is that we can concentrate on avoiding contributing to our sorrow with this negative narrative."

On the other hand, if regrets or other negative ideas begin to creep in concerning a terrible experience, Goodman advises us to examine the facts. "Is there any evidence to support these ideas?" Is there anything you can think of that makes things appear brighter? "You're not rejecting reality; rather, you're pointing out everything that exists simultaneously," Goodman adds. So, you lost your job—does this indicate you're awful at what you do? Is there proof that it had nothing to do with your performance? Perhaps your work performance has suffered due to circumstances beyond your control. Perhaps you weren't terrific at your career because it wasn't a good fit for your abilities and strengths, but that doesn't make you bad. By analyzing all of the facts, you'll be better equipped to discern what you have and don't have control over—and avoid allowing a difficult incident to define your self-worth.[23][24][25]

Dr. Gooden suggests that another strategy to counter our inner negative story is to ask ourselves where those ideas are coming from. Perhaps social media posts that elicit comparison might feed negative self-talk. Consider filtered Instagram photos from someone you haven't seen since high school that make you feel like your life pales compared to theirs or that you're somehow less deserving. Dr.

---

[23] "What Is Self-Awareness and Why Is It Important? [+5 Ways to Increase It]." 24 Apr. 2022, https://positivepsychology.com/self-awareness-matters-how-you-can-be-more-self-aware/.

[24] "Case Study: Becoming Self-Aware • Partnership for Public Service." https://ourpublicservice.org/public-service-leadership-institute/tools/case-study-becoming-self-aware/.

[25] "Self-Awareness Test: How Self-Aware Are You? - My Question Life." 04 May. 2020, https://myquestionlife.com/self-awareness-test/.

Gooden recommends asking yourself, "Where did that tale come from?" and "Is it true?" These questions may assist you in realizing that negative views about oneself are frequently the consequence of cultural or childhood indoctrination.

Dr. Solomon describes a mother with poor self-esteem who scolded herself when she made errors as an example of how we internalize the voice of a hypercritical parent. Or the parent who was eager to criticize his son's physical faults. Breaking intergenerational traditions is difficult, but it can also be a liberating step toward building self-love. "It's great to know that bad habits may be broken, such as being too judgmental of your body or talents," says Dr. Solomon.

It is not appropriate to blame our parents or caretakers for our lack of self-esteem. They likely tried their best while raising you, and you didn't get what you needed when you were little. "We are not accountable for how caretakers abused, misunderstood, or ignored us when we were young," Dr. Solomon explains. "However, as adults, we must examine and alter the coping techniques we created to deal with that grief." Again, she adds, learning to accept what occurred in the past so you can go on—perhaps with the support of a therapist if you're struggling on your own—may help you get closer to self-love.[26][27]

However, even if you don't feel those messages about your specific group are true about you, Dr. Gooden says there may be pressure to outperform to disprove them. "Some individuals begin to overlook

---

[26] "8 simple ways to practise self-love | Mental Health Foundation." 23 Oct. 2018, https://www.mentalhealth.org.uk/blog/8-simple-ways-practise-self-love.

[27] "How to Love Yourself: 6 Therapist-Backed Tips for Practicing Self-Love ...." 04 Mar. 2022, https://www.self.com/story/how-to-love-yourself.

their physical, emotional, and mental requirements in proving on an outer level that they're worthy and deserve respect," she adds.

It can also be difficult for trauma survivors, who frequently suffer from guilt and self-blame, to think they are deserving of love. When it comes to interpersonal trauma, such as sexual assault or other boundary violations, the underlying message is that you are unworthy of respect. "It's quite normal for trauma survivors to absorb that message and conclude, there must be something wrong with me if this person did this to me," says Dr. Gooden. Working through oppression and trauma on your own can be extremely difficult, so both Dr. Gooden and Dr. Solomon recommend working through these issues with a therapist, if possible—here's advice for finding a culturally competent therapist and some tips for finding an affordable one. Trying to be friendlier to our body, on the other hand, can be a modest step toward recovery. "When we value our bodies, we can alter our connection with them away from judgment and recognize that they—and we—are deserving of love and care," explains Dr. Gooden. She suggests relaxing self-care staples like having a warm bath with essential oils or scented candles or playing your favorite music and dancing it out in your living room. Your body-centered kindness, however, does not have to appear like that. Going on a walk, eating a good dinner, or wearing comfy jeans, for example, may appeal to you.

Practice Setting Boundaries

Setting healthy limits in relationships is a vital step toward developing self-love. Dr. Solomon recommends avoiding devoting your time and energy to those who make you feel unworthy, such as parents, friends, or relationships. "Part of practicing self-love is not looking for water in a dry well," she explains. "I advise making relationship and sexual decisions based on pleasure, comfort, safety, and communication."

Social media influencers may make self-love appear shallow or even poisonous (for example, employing "self-love" to avoid accepting responsibility for one's actions or attributing success to self-love rather than privilege). However, defining self-love as acceptance of who you are and a dedication to personal progress has the potential to have a dramatic influence on your life. "Self-love does not imply navel-gazing and never giving to the world." On the contrary, it's the ideal basis for a loving, healthy relationship with another person. Furthermore, it provides the finest basis for being a parent. "It's the finest basis for sharing your gifts globally," Dr. Gooden explains.[28][29]

---

[28] "Increase Clients' Self-Love: 30 Exercises, Techniques and Worksheets." 29 May. 2022, https://positivepsychology.com/self-love-exercises-worksheets/.
[29] "Self Love Quotes (3920 quotes) - Goodreads." https://www.goodreads.com/quotes/tag/self-love.

CHAPTER 2

Self-Love and Other People

When we think of self-love, we often imagine someone reading self-help books or embracing a tree; however, self-love is much more than that. Research has proven that self-love is essential for mental health and prevents despair and anxiety.

Modern civilization is structured so that we are compelled to compete with one another or even with ourselves. We strive to meet our short-term objectives and develop ourselves to meet societal standards. Every week, we slog in and out; even on weekends,' relaxing' and 'having a good time' feel like work.

As a result, we are overly hard on ourselves all too frequently without even realizing it. We're all busy with our job, social contacts, life objectives, weekend plans, etc. In a society that needs us to work, think, and act like programmed bots, love is the one thing that keeps us going and makes us less robotic. Everyone needs love, and we expend the majority of our efforts on loving others, whether they are friends, spouses, children, or relatives.[30][31][32]

We all want to spread happiness, but the issue is, do we make enough for ourselves? The idea of self-love comes into play since we can't always rely on others to provide us with the affection we need. Practicing self-love means that you don't have to rely on others to be happy, which is an empowering feeling. Put yourself first, and don't be too hard on yourself when you practice self-love. Let that tiny voice in your head go the next time it says, "You can never get it right," since it will only keep you from achieving your goals. When someone we care about makes a mistake, we are quick to forgive them, but we are often far too harsh with ourselves when it comes to our own mistakes.

The first step toward self-love is accepting that we are only human and that it is normal to make mistakes, lose at times, and not have the best day...week...or month. We have to love ourselves and let the negative things go; things will change, and terrible times will pass.

The first benefit of loving oneself is a greater sense of well-being. A more positive viewpoint on life may result from developing a deeper affection for oneself and, as a result, loving oneself more. The second advantage of self-love is that it can motivate us to develop healthy behaviors. Self-love entails caring for one's body, soul, and mind. As a result, people who love themselves typically hesitate to do things that would disrupt their peace of mind. As a result, it can

---

[30] "7 Examples of Self-Awareness (and Why It's so Important)." 03 May. 2022, https://www.trackinghappiness.com/why-self-awareness-important/.

[31] "15 signs you're more self-aware than you may think - Ideapod." 20 Oct. 2021, https://ideapod.com/signs-of-self-awareness/.

[32] "15 signs you're more self-aware than you may think - Ideapod." 20 Oct. 2021, https://ideapod.com/signs-of-self-awareness/.

assist us in developing healthy behaviors. If you start appreciating your body and mind more than others, you will not work on weekends; instead, you will go for a drive or do anything else that soothes your mind.[33][34]

Another significant advantage of self-love is improved mental health.

If you've had a difficult week, take the weekend off and go somewhere; disconnect from your phone and give yourself some time.[1] Consider yourself vital; cherish yourself as much as your friends and family. Happiness and self-love are inextricably linked, and we all have the right to be happy. The United Nations has issued a resolution on happiness, recognizing happiness and well-being as universal aspirations. As a result, we should seek to love ourselves and spread that love to others rather than strive for perfection. Self-love is the key to happiness, and a happy person is significantly more likely to succeed in all aspects of life.

Do you tell yourself that you adore yourself? Do you grin at yourself in the mirror? Do you make time for yourself during the day? These questions point to the same thing: a positive self-image founded on self-love. But unfortunately, we frequently prefer our caffeine, children, spouse, parents, career, and hobbies before ourselves. Learning to love yourself takes time and work, but the results are well worth it.

---

[33] "Self-love Definition & Meaning - Merriam-Webster." https://www.merriam-webster.com/dictionary/self-love.

[34] "13 Habits of Self-Love Every Woman Should Adopt - Healthline." 18 Sept. 2018, https://www.healthline.com/health/13-self-love-habits-every-woman-needs-to-have.

Acquire Life Satisfaction

When you truly love yourself, you develop an accepting mentality. You grow more inclined to accept your life stages and circumstances and accept responsibility for your actions. You also understand where love, happiness, passion, and honesty stem. When you recognize your power over your life, you become content with how you live it. Simply being content with your life has a significant mental influence, contributing to a lower-stress existence.

Develop Healthy Self-Esteem

You will build healthy self-esteem due to self-love, which is feeling good about yourself, your ideas, and your talents. Having high self-esteem implies that you recognize failure as a learning opportunity rather than a painful indication of loss. Your pride and confidence are not readily shaken when you appreciate your ideas and abilities. You will execute everyday jobs and activities without reluctance. Your self-esteem heavily influences your mental health. You'll be less likely to suffer from loneliness, alcohol misuse, or anxiety if you have a high sense of self-esteem.

Develop A Healthy Lifestyle

You'll want to give your body all it needs while on the path to loving yourself: sleep, food, water, and exercise. Most individuals find it difficult to live a healthy lifestyle, but it is possible to do so to achieve your goals. Self-love will motivate you to incorporate your objectives into your everyday routine. The good effects of your lifestyle will quickly become apparent as you gain the confidence to take on new tasks. Being appreciative, spending time alone, practicing mindfulness, accepting forgiveness, and wearing your confidence proudly are all advantages of creating good habits. When you love yourself, you will feel less anxious or uncomfortable when confronted with adversity. You will not compete with others or compare yourself to them. You will accept your difficulties. You'll have an optimistic mindset and be eager to be innovative and attempt new things.[35][36]

Self-confidence comes from believing in yourself and your skills. For example, you could be confident in one area, like cooking, dancing, or communicating, but nervous in another, like dancing or public speaking. On the other hand, self-esteem is concerned with how you perceive yourself. It all comes down to your self-esteem. Regardless of what occurs on the outside, do you love, care for, and respect yourself? It's easy to deceive yourself as a high achiever and believe you have self-esteem. As long as you perform and do well, everything is OK, right?

That is unless you don't. That's when it all goes downhill... I concluded this wasn't good enough for me when I discovered I considered myself less deserving, cool, and intriguing due to my external circumstances. It shouldn't be good enough for you if this resonates with you. As the saying goes, your worst breakdowns frequently lead to your greatest breakthroughs. So, I went to work. This time, instead of establishing my worth, I will practice self-love. Here are some of the most effective methods I've learned for doing precisely that:

---

[35] "Self Love – What it Actually Means: Misconceptions Shattered." 03 Mar. 2022, https://joannabel.com/self-love/.
[36] "Self-Care - Active Minds." https://www.activeminds.org/about-mental-health/self-care/.

Focus On Being Someone Who Loves

If you don't love yourself right now, it's difficult to make a quantum jump and become someone who does. Self-love, like muscular growth, requires constant practice. Rather than loving yourself, concentrate on being someone who loves. Allow love to flow through you as much as possible. Pay attention to what you like about the individuals you meet. While shopping, sitting in a meeting, or interacting with someone, think about what you appreciate. Locate as many things to love and admire as possible to acclimate your body to pleasant feelings.

When things go as planned, when we accomplish, and when people like us, it's simple to be kind toward ourselves, not so much when things go wrong, we make mistakes or are rejected. We tend to be the harshest on ourselves when we struggle the most. In those circumstances, consider how someone who adores you might behave. What do you think they'd say? What are they going to do? How would they act? They are unlikely to criticize, judge, or berate you. They'd show you love, sympathy, and acceptance. If you cannot recall a specific person or memory, consider how the most loving human would treat you. Then practice becoming like that to yourself.

Stop Comparing Yourself

Comparison suffocates self-love. And we're not typically that polite when it comes to making comparisons, are we? Instead, we compare our biggest shortcomings to someone else's greatest achievement. In a nutshell, you're condemned to fail. Instead, recognize that you are the author of your tale. Recognize that you can't compare your life to someone else's since you never know how they feel or how they see their lives, no matter how well you know them. Instead, devote your time and attention to nurturing and constructing your path.[37][38]

Desires are quite powerful. To take action and make those aspirations a reality is to honor and care for oneself. By performing everyday acts, you demonstrate that you are deserving of the life you seek. It doesn't have to be a big deal—just little and persistent moves in the direction of joy, caring, and enthusiasm. This shows that you care for and appreciate your dreams, and hence yourself. Is there ever a better moment to do so than now?

Ask Your Guidance System for Help

Consider your emotions to be your guide. When you feel good about yourself, it suggests your thoughts are in sync with how your soul/higher self-views you. When you feel horrible about yourself, it's a warning flag that you need to adjust your outlook. How does it feel to consider a notion like "I am [something you dislike about yourself]"? Probably not so wonderful, isn't it? Then it's time to think about something else. Replace it with something gentler. "I'm simply so lost and bewildered," for example, might be substituted with "I'm doing my best to go ahead."

Oh, this is significant! You've probably heard Jim Rohn's famous quote: "You are the average of the five people you spend the most time with." Consider who those folks are right now. Do they motivate you, fill you up, and desire the best for you? You don't have

---

[37] "5 Self-Care Practices for Every Area of Your Life - Verywell Mind." 23 May. 2022, https://www.verywellmind.com/self-care-strategies-overall-stress-reduction-3144729.

[38] "Self-Care: 12 Ways to Take Better Care of Yourself." 28 Dec. 2018, https://www.psychologytoday.com/us/blog/click-here-happiness/201812/self-care-12-ways-take-better-care-yourself.

to keep spending time together because you've been friends. Choose who you spend your time with carefully—don't give it away in the name of kindness. (That's not polite to you or the other person.) Be there because you want to, not because you have to. When we fail, make a mistake, or are rejected, we frequently become even more critical of ourselves. Is it appropriate to beat someone who is lying down? No, not at all. Instead, choose to be the most loving and forgiving of yourself when things do not go as planned. When you trip and fall. When you say the incorrect things. When you are rejected, or a project fails. Ask yourself what you require, and then shower it on yourself.

Make Room for Healthy Habits

Yes, yes, yes! Begin caring for yourself by reflecting on what you eat, exercise, and do with your time. Do things not to "get it done" or "have to," but because you care about yourself. Don't want to go to the gym? Then listen to a soul-calming podcast and go for a stroll. Create good habits, not just cognitively but also emotionally.

Postpone Your Worry and Negative Thoughts

Are you ready for a fantastic tip? If this is the case, then get thrilled. A "worry-free month" is a fantastic method I recently learned (I named it myself). Consider how much of your anxiety genuinely benefits you. Sure, part of our anxiety has a purpose in that it serves as a wake-up call when we need to get our sh*t together and start acting. However, I believe that 97 percent of it is unnecessary. When those ideas arise, remind yourself, "Thank you, but I'll deal with this next month." You cease feeding negative ideas and slow down their momentum by telling your mind that you'll deal with it later (and when). Then you just keep doing it month after month.[39,40]

Accept What You Cannot Love

This may have been the most significant game-changer for me. Because let's face it, it's simple to love what you like in yourself and difficult to love what you don't. So, instead of attempting to appreciate those bits, which would most likely leave you thinking, "Are you kidding me?" focus on tolerating them. Going to the shop, for example, might be tough. Rather than rejecting or attempting to cherish this anxious aspect of myself, I am telling myself to accept it. When this happens, I tell myself something like, "It's alright, I'll feel frightened going to the grocery today." It doesn't mean the end of the world." To build self-love, you don't have to adore everything about yourself; all you need is acceptance. When anything happens that makes you want to criticize yourself, consider it practice for accepting what is. There are ups and downs in life. The disease can develop from good health. Successes sometimes devolve into failures. Romantic love has the potential to turn chilly. However, regardless of what occurs on the outside, we may still have a strong foundation based on self-love. In today's world, self-love is not a luxury; it is necessary. So, begin applying some of the behaviors mentioned earlier, and most importantly, be kind to yourself when you fall short. Then just brush yourself off and get back into it. As the saying goes, practice makes perfect. Finally, understand that you

---

[39] "What Is Self-Care and Why Is It Critical for Your Health?." 19 May. 2021, https://www.everydayhealth.com/self-care/.
[40] "Self-Care: Definition and Examples - Verywell Health." 04 Jan. 2022, https://www.verywellhealth.com/self-care-definition-and-examples-5212781.

are caring for the planet by caring for yourself. Your actions have an impact on others.

However, one of the most powerful and significant things you can do in life is learn to love yourself. Your heart is your source of power, and when you become the source of love in your own life, everything changes. Your relationships, work, and health bloom when you learn to love yourself. We prefer to think of self-love as an art form that can be studied and developed over time at Project Love. We create a loving and healthy connection with ourselves when we practice self-love, and something miraculous happens — we become our own best friends. Here are some simple methods to begin practicing the art of self-love right away:

Nourish Yourself

If you're new to the practice of self-love, begin by concentrating on nourishing yourself. Nourishing your body is the most fundamental kind of self-love, so this week, be conscious of what you put in your body – give it what it craves. Begin your day with a green smoothie, then indulge in a raw chocolate snack before preparing a nutritious meal packed with superfoods. Our eating habits reflect how much we love ourselves. So, practice self-care, and you'll establish solid foundations for self-love.

Take Yourself Out on A Date

Make this the month you go on a date with yourself if you've never done so before. Solo dating is all about spending time with yourself and doing something unique for yourself. When it comes to practicing self-love is one of the most powerful (and enjoyable) things you can do. By doing something special for yourself that you would ordinarily do for someone else, you give yourself the love and attention you typically offer to others. Finally, you've turned your affection on yourself. Anything from a cup of coffee and some cake to a weekend at the spa has worked for our clients. Whatever they do, they always come away humming.

Start A Gratitude Journal

It has been established that simply writing down 5 things you are grateful for each day will educate your brain to be more optimistic, resulting in an overall sensation of happiness. It is an important tool for practicing self-love since it requires us to adopt an attitude of appreciation, love, and abundance. So, get yourself a notepad and, for the next week, at the end of each day, write down some things you're grateful for and see how nice it feels to conclude your day this way. And in addition to offering thanks for what occurred to you that day and the people in your life for whom you are grateful, include yourself in your thankfulness practice. Find at least one thing to praise yourself for every day, and your connection with yourself will transform into an extraordinarily loving one.

Make Your Body Happy

When learning to love ourselves, we must devote a significant amount of time and attention to our bodies. How we feel in our bodies directly impacts how we feel in ourselves. Our dissociation with our bodies frequently causes loneliness and a lack of affection. You want to maintain that beautiful body of yours energized and full of vigor. As part of your self-love regimen, do activities that make you feel good in your body, whether yoga, running, 80's Aerobics, or dancing like Beyonce (a personal favorite)!

Express Yourself

It's critical to discover methods to express oneself and feel free to be completely yourself truly. Everyone has something that they enjoy doing: dancing, writing, singing, painting, acting, sculpting, cooking, producing music, drawing, DJ'ing, ceramics, or poetry. It's something we do as kids all the time. It's always something that brings us back to life.[41][42][43]

So, how does it work for you? When do you feel, you can completely let go and be yourself? If it's not something you do right now, consider it in the past. What brings you to life and allows you to connect with the deepest elements of yourself? Make time for it in your life now. Whether it's channeling your inner Rihanna on the dance floor, singing like no one is listening, or painting in large, strong brush strokes for the sake of painting, you must find time to do the activities that allow you to express yourself from the heart truly.[44]

Write A Loving Letter to Yourself

In the same way, you would write a letter to someone you care about, write to yourself. Make a list of all the things and people in your life that make you happy right now, and express your gratitude for them in your essay. If you're feeling low, give yourself a pep talk,

---

[41] "What Self-Awareness Really Is (and How to Cultivate It)." 04 Jan. 2018, https://hbr.org/2018/01/what-self-awareness-really-is-and-how-to-cultivate-it.

[42] "7 Tips for Improving Your Self-Awareness | Psych Central." 05 May. 2022, https://psychcentral.com/health/how-to-be-more-self-aware-and-why-its-important.

[43] "What Is Self-Awareness, and How Do You Get It? | Psychology Today." 11 Mar. 2019, https://www.psychologytoday.com/us/blog/click-here-happiness/201903/what-is-self-awareness-and-how-do-you-get-it.

[44] "Self Care 101 | Psychology Today." 27 May. 2018, https://www.psychologytoday.com/us/blog/skinny-revisited/201805/self-care-101.

and jot down your future ambitions and dreams. Think about what advice and encouragement you can give yourself at this time, and then write a letter to yourself that you're proud of and that you'd like to send out to the world. Wait for your letter to come in the mail a few days later!

Shower Yourself in Feel-Good Vibes

We have considerably more ability than we realize to create the sensations we want to have in life, regardless of where we are or what is happening. We only need to learn how to access those sensations. Find a photo of yourself from a point in your life when you felt full of pleasure, contentment, serenity, or satisfaction - whatever you want to feel – and look at it whenever you want to be reminded of how you felt. Put the photo somewhere you'll see it every day: make it your phone's screensaver or print it out and hang it on your bathroom mirror. Take a peek at that photo whenever you need a pick-me-up and soak in those feel-good sensations.

Self-care is how we look after our mental, emotional, and physical wellness. The things we engage in allow us to remain our best selves. Self-care is an action-oriented approach for us to express our love for ourselves. Loving oneself is exactly what it sounds like. It entails embracing all elements of oneself, including your flaws, shortcomings, and things you don't necessarily like about yourself. It is also about having high expectations for your pleasure and well-being.[45][46]

---

[45] "What is self-care? | Global Self-Care Federation."
https://www.selfcarefederation.org/what-is-self-care.
[46] "Self-care tips: The complete guide to taking care of yourself."
https://www.tonyrobbins.com/mental-health/self-care-tips/.

Many individuals are unfamiliar with the notions of self-care and self-love. After all, we are frequently taught that prioritizing yourself or your wants is selfish and that you should devote your efforts to others. However, practicing self-love does not imply that you are selfish or a narcissist; you will not accept less than you deserve because you understand and respect your needs. Self-care and self-love frequently simply entail offering the same respect and care that you give for others to yourself. We've all heard the adage "treat people the way you want to be treated." However, while considering self-love and self-care, it is frequently necessary to examine the inverse. Treat yourself with the same care and grace that you show to your friends, family, and loved ones. We are frequently much gentler with our loved ones than with ourselves.

We are typically our own worst critics, as the cliché goes. Self-love requires abandoning that adage and moving forward by establishing an atmosphere for yourself in which you may make errors, grow, and thrive. Self-love is a wonderful aim to strive for, but it may be difficult to attain in reality, especially if you are not in the habit of practicing self-care. Self-care is a discipline that, over time, can lead to increased self-love. Self-love will not come quickly, especially if you are coming from a position of self-hatred, harsh criticism, perfectionism, etc. Still, it may be gradually absorbed into your life via persistent acts of self-care. Incorporating self-care into your routine in simple, manageable stages can boost your self-kindness, self-love, and general humanity.

Steps To Practice Self Love Everyday

Recognizing And Accepting Your Emotional State

Nobody is always content. They are not always optimistic or the best version of themselves. Holding oneself to fair standards is an important aspect of self-love. You must accept that some days will be better than others and that it is perfectly normal to have a bad day, week, or even slump time. It's critical to regularly assess your emotional state so that you can recognize and accept your emotions. In practice, this means not behaving as though everything is OK when you know it isn't. "It's nothing," alternatively, "I'm OK," is a phrase that irritates many people. Don't play the same games over and over again. So that you can behave and prepare appropriately, pay attention to your emotional state![47][48][49]

You must not only acknowledge your emotional condition but also accept it. Tailoring your goals or routine to your current emotional state is an important aspect of accepting your emotional state. Checking in with your emotional state is the foundation of any excellent self-care program. It is also critical to detect whether a slump has lasted too long. While it is necessary to give yourself some slack, take some time off, or completely give in to a poor mood now and again, it is also crucial to recognize that our behaviors, habits, and routines may significantly impact our moods! If you're in a rut, think about how you may adjust your routine in a good way to get back into the groove. Self-care is frequently a combination of giving

---

[47] "Self-aware - definition of self-aware by The Free Dictionary." https://www.thefreedictionary.com/self-aware.

[48] "The True Meaning of Self-Awareness (& How to Tell If You're Actually ...." 11 May. 2018, https://blog.hubspot.com/marketing/self-awareness.

[49] "Self-Awareness: Why It's Good for You and How to Develop It." 21 Apr. 2022, https://psychcentral.com/health/self-awareness.

oneself love and forgiveness while also keeping positive behaviors that actively strive to boost your mood.

Take Time for Yourself

All extroverts (and introverts), take note! As enjoyable as it is to be with others and socialize, it is essential to analyze your mental condition (the importance of which we discussed above) and devote some time to self-care. Many people overextend themselves between jobs, everyday life, and social responsibilities. And we understand that having a nice social event to look forward to frequently helps individuals get through the week.

After all, who doesn't appreciate a nice Wednesday night plan to get them over the hump day? However, these social gatherings mustn't interfere with your much-needed me-time. It might be tough for persons with acute FOMO to pass down a nice night out or a movie with friends. However, sometimes things that you would normally like are taxing because you should have used that leisure time to ponder inside and practice self-care. We're not saying you should disregard your social calendar but rather set aside time to do activities that will help you recharge. This may necessitate scheduling time to recuperate! Though getting this alone time in your hectic life may be the most difficult aspect, you mustn't squander it![50][51]

Don't waste self-care time looking through your phone or passively watching TV! Take some time (even if it's only a few minutes!) to

---

[50] "What is Self-Care? - Habits for Wellbeing." 07 Jun. 2014, https://www.habitsforwellbeing.com/what-is-self-care/.
[51] "A guide to self-care - Life in Mind Australia." https://lifeinmind.org.au/research/self-care.

engage in mindfulness practices, and anything else helps you tune into your emotions. This may be going to a weekly yoga class, going for a stroll after work, downloading a meditation app, or starting a diary. There is no incorrect method to exercise self-care if you undertake activities that help you relax and feel centered. It is not selfish to prioritize alone time to focus on self-love; it is necessary for your self-care regimen. Keeping at home nowadays means staying protected.

Get Enough Sleep

Sleep is crucial, yet it is often disregarded in this day and age. People's sleep cycles are frequently disrupted when overly busy and anxious. When you have a lot on your plate, it's easy to justify staying up late and getting up early simply to get everything done. Getting enough sleep is the bedrock of all wellness! In addition to getting adequate sleep, pay attention to the quality of your sleep. Developing a nighttime routine is an excellent first step in increasing the quantity and quality of your sleep. Several sleep applications are available on the market that may help you track your sleep and fall asleep.

Exercising

Physical activity significantly impacts our moods and physical and mental health. Therefore, maintaining your physical health is an important element of self-care since it ensures that your body is operating correctly and serving you.

Exercise can increase endorphins and assist us in releasing the tension that accumulates in our daily lives. If you are stressed, adding another task (such as going to the gym) to your to-do list may seem daunting. On the other hand, it may be as easy as going for a walk during your lunch break or doing yoga for 30 minutes (there are apps for that!) when you return home. Developing a regimen that integrates exercise into your everyday life can help you maintain your mental and physical health and progress on your road to self-love.[52][53][54]

It might be scary to go on a mile-long run or sign up for a yoga session if you are not used to exercising. Remember to set fair goals for yourself and ease into a more active lifestyle. If you push yourself too hard at first, you will likely become discouraged and give up on exercise entirely. Instead, gradually include more exercise into your daily routine and work your way to more rigorous activities. For example, instead of using the elevator, you may choose the furthest parking spot or arrive at your destination a few stops earlier than required to acquire a walk-in.

Eating Right

How can you expect to be your best self if you are miserable? Paying attention to your nutrition is a crucial element of self-care since it affects how you feel and how much energy you have. You may work out all you want, but if all you eat is trash, there's no way you'll feel well or be in excellent physical health. Also, eating properly might make it a LOT simpler to exercise because it provides more energy. Eating healthily does not necessitate constant dieting! It's not so much about your weight as how you feel. Pay attention to items that

---

[52] "What Is Self-Awareness? (And How To Increase Yours)." 09 Sept. 2021, https://www.indeed.com/career-advice/career-development/what-is-self-awareness.
[53] "Self-awareness - Wikipedia." https://en.wikipedia.org/wiki/Self-awareness.
[54] "What Is Self-Awareness, and Why Is It Important? - BetterUp." 21 Apr. 2021, https://www.betterup.com/blog/what-is-self-awareness.

irritate your stomach (many individuals have food intolerances that they are entirely unaware of!) and aim to include all of your major food categories. Eating well can also improve your mental health. Eating nutritious meals can improve your short-term memory; thus, brain foods exist! Eating fatty fish, almonds, leafy greens, and antioxidant-rich foods (blueberries, acai berries) is good for your health and can boost your brain function. Whether you order in or cook together, embarking on a nutrition journey may bring you and your spouse closer. Try Relish free for 7 days to learn more about becoming healthy and feeling wonderful in your relationship.

Using Self-Talk

Learning to participate in positive self-talk is an important component of your self-care journey. Self-talk is the mental dialogue that runs through our thoughts most of the time. We do self-talk unknowingly, frequently reflective of our subconscious ideas and sentiments. As a result, our self-talk may be quite negative at times, leading to emotions of self-doubt, self-judgment, and even self-loathing. Don't worry if your self-talk narrative is overly negative; there are mindfulness techniques you may employ to modify your inner conversation to be more positive.[55]

Giving oneself positive affirmations is a simple and effective technique to do this. What qualities do you admire in yourself? What are you particularly proud of? Reminding yourself of these things regularly (for example, when brushing your teeth in the morning) will put you in a more optimistic frame of mind, naturally inspiring positive self-talk. Recognizing when you are engaging in

---

[55] "What Is Self-Care? - Healthline." 03 Sept. 2019, https://www.healthline.com/health-news/self-care-is-not-just-treating-yourself.

negative self-talk is a crucial component of using self-talk to your advantage; if you see this, attempt to identify the source and proceed in a forgiving and positive manner.

Challenging A Negative Story About Yourself

When we allow negative self-talk to go unchecked for too long, we might build negative narratives about ourselves that can be extremely destructive to our self-esteem. We eventually internalize these negative narratives about ourselves, and before we realize it, these tales have changed our attitudes and even our behaviors.

To get to the bottom of the issue, you must first discover the negative tales you tell yourself about yourself. Where do these unfavorable reports originate? Next, you must determine why you continue to believe these bad stories. You can help disrupt the negative thought loop propagating negative self-talk if you can discover why, you are telling yourself these tales. You may use the same positive self-talk tactics outlined above to fight these negative tales. Finally, begin showcasing the positive aspects of yourself to internalize a positive narrative. Try our award-winning relationship training app instead of letting self-doubt and insecurities damage your relationship. Begin your 7-day free trial now!

Forgiving Yourself

This entails practicing self-compassion. We all make errors, large and little, and while they may feel monumental at the moment, they aren't. Life goes on, and you should too. Accepting self-compassion allows you to look back on your acts with love, empathy, and support, allowing you to forgive yourself for whatever happened.

Nursing a grudge against oneself can be as harmful as holding a grudge against someone else.[56][57]

Grudges need to retain a tremendous quantity of negative energy, which may be quite draining. Forgiveness allows you to release negative sentiments about yourself or your acts, freeing up your energy and emotional capacity to embrace more loving conduct.

Committing To Self-Love

Achieving self-love may be a long process that does not come immediately. It might take a long time to break harmful behaviors that drive us to be cruel to ourselves. It is critical to realize that this procedure will require time and dedication. Self-love does not require immediate pleasure. Most of us know how to give ourselves a pick-me-up, whether it's ice cream, a cute new outfit, or binge-watching a couple of episodes of our favorite program. And while these activities are enjoyable and should be continued, they are not long-term paths to self-kindness and self-love. Don't forget to enjoy the little things along the way, but remember that awareness and devotion are key to success.

Commit To Learning More

Words like self-care and mindfulness seem to be everywhere these days, which is fantastic as we all learn to be more reflective and tolerant of ourselves. However, this is a new trend, implying that additional research and procedures are being developed. Committing to testing new self-care routes and continuing to learn

---

[56] "What Is Self-Awareness and How Does It Develop?." 14 Jul. 2020, https://www.verywellmind.com/what-is-self-awareness-2795023.
[57] "Self-aware Definition & Meaning - Merriam-Webster." https://www.merriam-webster.com/dictionary/self-aware.

as these ideas evolve should be an important part of your self-care journey. We may always learn to be more compassionate and kinder to ourselves. Keeping up with the most recent research on the issue will help you develop novel approaches to care for yourself! Read a book, get a new mindfulness app, or look for online communities that promote self-care strategies. Engaging with new resources will educate you more about how to care for your mental, physical, and emotional well-being.

CHAPTER 3

Reconnecting with Your Body

Looking after your mental health is sometimes thought to be something you do in your brain – attempting to think your way to a happy place. However, the body-mind link is one of the most underappreciated methods to improve well-being. Sadly, many of us feel conflicted about our bodies and don't pay attention to the changes below the collarbone. So here are some pointers on linking your body and mind for your advantage. We might become so preoccupied with how it seems that we lose sight of all the body's benefits. The brain is a sophisticated computer that controls everything; the stomach supplies energy, your skin protects you, and your feet and arms transport you. What do you appreciate about your body?

It's all too easy to become fixated on our flaws and overlook our strengths. So, try standing in front of a mirror (naked if you're brave) and listing five things you appreciate about your physique. Do you have nice hair? Soft skin? Elegant digits? Beautiful eyes? Cello-like curves? Long limbs? What do you appreciate about your physical appearance? Learn about what's going on in your body. The body scan is a mindfulness exercise that assists you in tuning into your internal environment, including physical and emotional experiences. If anything has disturbed you, it's an excellent method to calm down and center yourself. Lie down, take a few deep breaths, and begin with one of your feet, feeling deeper into the body — muscles, bones, blood flow.[58][59]

Is it hot or chilly outside? Are you tense or relaxed? Is it numb or tingling? Pay attention to what is present without criticizing it as you scan your body from your toes to the top of your head. Tal Ben-Shahar, a Harvard psychologist, once stated that not exercising is equivalent to taking antidepressants. When you're sad, it might be difficult to regulate your mood. This is where your body can assist you in feeling better quickly. Moving your body releases endorphins, making you feel good without mental gymnastics. The trick is to accomplish something enjoyable rather than something unpleasant. Take a stroll, dance, garden, or jump on a trampoline - whatever makes you happy.

Using the breath is one of the simplest methods to link the body and mind. If you're anxious, breathing deeply into your abdomen can function as a brake, bringing your body out of the 'fight or flight' reaction and into a state of calm. Abdominal breathing has several advantages, including reducing anxiety and sadness, increasing happiness and optimism, improving your capacity to handle emotions, and reducing impulsive behavior. Four-seven-eight

---

[58] "What Is Self-Care & Why Is Caring About Yourself Important?" https://thelawofattraction.com/self-care-tips/.
[59] "30 Self-Care Habits for a Strong and Healthy Mind, Body and Spirit." https://www.lifehack.org/834747/self-care.

breathing is one technique based on yoga practice. Inhale through the nose for four counts, hold for seven, and then exhale through the mouth for eight counts.

What exactly does it mean to be in touch with your body? Connection is defined as a two-way interaction between your mind and your body that is open and welcoming. This bond is critical for sex and our interactions with others. Getting information from our bodies about what's going on and what it signifies allows us to have more complete, meaningful life experiences.

What Is Disconnection Like?

It's difficult to express the lack of anything; however, here are some real-life examples:

- During sex, you're frequently 'in your brain,' finding thoughts more difficult to ignore than body sensations, decreasing desire. This may be truer at times than at others.
- If your spouse asks you what you appreciate about sex, you may be unclear about how to express the sensations or the type of touch you prefer. You could find it difficult to distinguish between positive and negative events.
- You may have noticed a decrease in your interest in sex or other enjoyable activities but are unsure why. If you've lost touch with what makes these activities enjoyable, you're unlikely to be driven to participate!
- You might not be able to relate how you feel to how you behave quickly. For example, you may have snapped at someone without realizing it until later.

- When someone asks you how you're feeling (rather than when you could instantly answer 'Fine!') And?'), you could find it difficult to pin down or identify the character of the experience. It may require some effort to articulate what is going on 'internally.'

It is unlikely to be constant if you feel separation like this; there may be moments when dissociation is more intense and others when connecting with your body is easier. Everyone goes through moments of separation; sometimes, they are necessary for coping with or surviving specific events. The difficulty arises when you become stuck in them, and they begin to limit your life experience.

What Causes Disconnection?

Disconnecting from your body is not a sign of personal failure; it is a simple development habit. Here are several scenarios that may have resulted in reduced connection with your body:

- You may have been through a traumatic incident. This is a reaction to our system being overburdened by a terrifying encounter. It might cause heightened sensitivity to physical and mental experiences, allowing you to become overwhelmed more readily. Disconnection from physical and emotional sensations is an innate response to shield you from difficult-to-control feelings. This is more likely if you haven't had the time or space to recuperate from what happened fully.
- A difficult relationship with your body. You may have gotten alienated from your body, as you might from a tough

relationship, due to illness, having a body linked with stigma or difference, or other circumstances. It may feel like a lot of work to get over the confusing sentiments, and why disturb things if you're surviving well?

- You may not have had the opportunity to tune into your body and sensations when you were younger. Perhaps you were pushed to move beyond tough sentiments quickly and get on with your life, or you were punished for displaying emotional responses. You may have learned to dull these and not express them in this atmosphere.

- To deal and move on from a terrible event, you may have discovered that it was simpler to avoid feelings. This may have become a habit because it was useful for a while over time.

It might be difficult to pinpoint when the gap began (or whether it has always existed) or what caused it. That's OK; comprehension isn't always required. However, if you suspect it was distressing or traumatic (or even if you're unsure), it's critical to be kind to yourself as you work to reestablish that connection. Connecting with complicated or challenging sentiments can be painful, and moving at your own pace is essential; otherwise, you'll reinforce that you and your feelings and experiences don't deserve to be treated seriously.

Before we begin, if any of these exercises are overwhelming, anxiety-inducing, or otherwise challenging for you, you must pause and give yourself time to feel calm and normal again. This might indicate that you've tapped into something particularly unpleasant for you, which is OK - this is your body protecting you. We may train ourselves to be more aware of what is going on in our bodies. It may be simpler for you to do it simultaneously every day or during an activity when you won't be bothered for a while. A shower or bath might be a nice place to start. Here are a few suggestions:

- One by one, become aware of your pulse at various spots on your body. You may be able to feel your pulse in your temples, mouth, wrists, groin, and ankles, among other places.
- Make a list of five items you're aware of and speak them aloud as you observe them. Things you can see, taste, smell, hear, and feel might be included. For example, 'I am aware of the light from the window; I am aware of the water on my skin, and I am aware of the buzzing of the bathroom fan.'
- Perform a body scan, noticing what you feel in each part of your body as you go gently from your toes to the top of your head. If moving each portion is a little help, go ahead! Even if you can't name the sensation or experience, try to stay with it for a second before moving on.

You should also take note of your reaction to doing this. Do you notice any of your sentiments changing once you focus on them? Do you have any ideas that come to mind when performing it? Do you see any patterns? Name feelings allow you to communicate with others about your feelings and acknowledge your emotions to yourself, which may be empowering. Finally, try to find words to summarize what you felt at the end of a body scan or other noticing activity. Say them aloud, write them down, or confide in a partner or friend if you trust them with this.

Non-Judgment

A critical component of this is not judging what you notice. People might be quite quick to believe that they should be feeling or not feeling anything, particularly (though not always) when dealing with painful emotions such as grief, guilt, and rage. However, this judgment typically causes the disconnect in the first place; telling ourselves that we can't or shouldn't behave in this manner may lead to our ignoring ourselves and our needs. If you see yourself evaluating an emotion, do the following:

- Recognize it! Even if it's only for yourself. 'I saw I was exhausted.' I couldn't figure out why, and I felt horrible; I should have a solid reason to be exhausted.'
- Return your attention to the sensation you're experiencing rather than the judgment. Consider that for a moment.
- Continue to the next experience. If you find yourself clinging to that judgment, later on, it may be worthwhile to investigate why. What was so terrible with the very normal emotion you had?[60][61]

Bring It All Together

The next stage is to see whether you can put this into effect in your daily life. As an example:

---

[60] "What Is Self-Care? 30 Best Self Care Ideas, Activities and Apps." 02 Sept. 2021, https://parade.com/1039023/allisonscerbomusante/what-is-self-care/.

[61] "Self-Care: What It Really Is and How to Do It Well." 27 Apr. 2020, https://nickwignall.com/self-care/.

1. Speaking with others about how you're feeling. This might be about dealing with a difficult situation, such as informing your spouse that you've discovered you're particularly apprehensive about sex.

2. Being kind to yourself - if you see yourself suffering from some uncomfortable feelings, this might be a clue that you need to look after yourself rather than just 'get on with things.'

3. Noticing and boosting enjoyment - if you can begin to tune into concepts and sensations that feel good for you, you may discover methods to do them more and ask others to assist you.

4. Standing up for yourself - It becomes simpler to assert your sentiments to others if you develop the practice of noticing and taking them seriously.

You may comprehend what needs to be addressed in your life by listening to your body. Your body can warn you when you're on the verge of burnout, defend you from illness, and reveal you when you're living outside your real purpose. Every day, your body gives you messages. How effectively do you detect and interpret your body's signals? Exhaustion, disease, worry, stress, and tension are all signals from your body that something needs to be addressed. Perhaps you have an underlying health problem, are not expressing your truth, or are in the wrong position or working too hard.

Your body communicates with you in three ways: initially as a whisper, then as a yell, and last as a shutdown if left unaddressed. Many people find it difficult to tune in and listen to their body's wisdom. Do you pay attention to your body's whispers? Or do you wait until your body provides unambiguous indications, such as an illness, a health risk, or exhaustion, before paying attention? I had health issues in my twenties when I was diagnosed with a chronic health condition. My body was cycling through burnout crashes, but I simply continued pushing to meet my academic objectives. Being chronically ill for seven years taught me the importance of paying attention when your body sends you signals. Despite having had my health difficulties in the past and understanding what I require to be healthy and prosper, I still find it difficult to honor my body's warnings at times. Only this year, I experienced another round of tiredness and burnout, which made me wonder, "How can it be so difficult to connect with and listen to our bodies' wisdom?"

The Struggle to Stay Connected

Slowing down long enough to observe your body's feelings and tune into the signals it's sending you might lead to resistance. You may be unwilling to listen to what your body is saying; sometimes, your body's wisdom is to slow down when you want to speed up, say no when you want to say Yes, or make changes that challenge the status quo. When you can face your opposition, you are better positioned to go through it and build a more enjoyable and easy-going existence. You may design a life in which you are not pushing yourself to the maximum and ignoring critical indications from your body.

Stress And Pressure

When you're stressed, your brain is geared to focus on the most pressing difficulties. This might result in you being detached from your body and failing to notice the signs it sends you. Regaining your calm by engaging your parasympathetic nervous system might assist you in reconnecting with how your body is experiencing. The easiest method to get out of your thoughts and back into your body is to take long, deep inhalations and exhalations. You may have normalized your experiences due to being under continual stress. Daily headaches may be the norm, five hours of sleep may be the norm, and dragging oneself through the day is no longer unusual. It's critical to recognize stress to respond early because stress causes inflammation in the body, leading to major illnesses and diseases such as heart disease, diabetes, and dementia.

Societal Expectations and Judgement

While you may understand the importance of listening to your body, we all have a critical voice in our thoughts that tells us, "You should be doing more," or "Keep going, keep pushing!" Glennon Doyle discusses the hurdles she experienced on her road to listening to her body in her book Untamed. She claims she believed that "sitting is laziness, and laziness is rude." Worthiness and kindness are achieved through hustle." She opted to change her belief after realizing it was no longer benefitting her or her relationships. "Hard labor is essential." Play and inactivity are also undesirable. My existence rather than my activity determines my worth. "I am deserving of relaxation," she writes. In our hustle-obsessed culture that emphasizes pushing through, it may be tough to live a mindful life, rest when you need it, experience guilt-free leisure, and respect your body's boundaries. Moving away from a hustling mentality, on the other hand, will help you to hear better and honor your body's demands and knowledge.

Personality And Passion

Being completely focused and passionate about your profession may often impede physical connection. Do you have trouble getting out of your mind and into your body? Do you prefer logic over emotion? Do you frequently ignore your body's cues to stop, often against what's best for you? I unquestionably fit within this group. Because I enjoy what I do, I am prone to overworking. I like being in my thoughts over being in my body. I like studying, researching, writing, and experimenting with new ideas. Even when my body tells me it's time, it may be difficult to take myself away from my creative efforts. Too frequently, I push through and keep working despite a building headache, stiff shoulders, or tiredness. According to neuroscience studies, an overworked brain is less efficient, but time away fosters creativity, productivity, and well-being. While you may be driven to work hard and have a strong desire to fulfill your mission, you perform your best work when you create more space and take time to relax and reset regularly.

Building Your Body Intelligence

"Body intelligence comprises the capacity to connect with our body's feelings or cues; listen to them, and respond to promote our overall function and quality of life," says body awareness specialist Thea O'Connor. "A fantastic method to grow awareness of internal signals from our body, also known as our 'interoceptive awareness,' is to start with the extremely basic items, every day," she says in her blog article "10 ways to listen to your body." "Develop a basic daily routine that grounds you in your body and allows you a minute to check-in," she advises. You could, for example, complete a basic Body Scan when you get up, then again at lunch and bedtime."[62][63]

Increasing my bodily awareness has been crucial in regaining my energy and health. I've returned to listening to my body and altering my regular habits. It has meant sleeping in more, resting when my body requires it, taking gentle walks instead of completing rigorous gym exercises, spending more time cooking healthy food, meditating, and returning to yin and restorative yoga. Every morning, I begin my day by asking myself, "How am I feeling today?" This question enables me to begin my day with bodily awareness. Some days, I feel great thankfulness and lightness, and I go about my day, noting all the small details that make my life so lovely. On other days, I'm exhausted and stressed. On those days, I present differently and proceed through the day more gently and compassionately.

Responding with Self-Compassion

When my body and mind are straining, I ask myself, "How can I make this easier?" I seek the road of least resistance. I've discovered that doing things the easy way might lead to feelings of guilt and shame. "Easy is lazy," says the conditioned voice in my brain, and "You should be trying more." I do my best to make room for that

---

[62] "What is Self-Care? - ISF." https://isfglobal.org/what-is-self-care/.
[63] "Self-Care Tips | Agency for Integrated Care - AIC." https://www.aic.sg/caregiving/self-care-tips.

voice while still honoring my body. Increasing my body awareness has involved more than just incorporating additional body-based practices into my weekly routine. It's all about altering my whole connection with my body. Instead of attempting to ignore my body's messages, I am now actively seeking direction from it and growing faith in its wisdom.

When I'm having a bad day and just want to get through it, I look to my body for solutions. "What do you need right now?" I ask my body. "You're weary; you need more coffee!" says my brain. When I ask my body, it responds with phrases like "Jess, you need to lie down for 15 minutes" or "You need fresh air and a stroll around the block." My body's speech is always more compassionate, nurturing, and gentle than my mind's voice. My inner voice may be a harsh taskmaster. Your body encourages you to cultivate greater self-compassion, self-love, and self-acceptance. After following my body's guidance, I feel healthier, more restored, and more creative.

You may also use your body's knowledge to create more aligned life choices that benefit your health and happiness. "The next time you have a decision to make that you are hesitant about: come to stillness, raise your question to yourself, then pick one option," O'Connor writes in her blog article, "3 strategies to establish confidence in your body." Take note of the visceral reaction you have in your body to that option. What does feeling stressed or uneasy tell you? What does it mean to be energized and expanded? Learning to recognize 'yes' and 'no' in your body is a valuable life skill with several applications." Reconnecting with your body starts with awareness and permission to slow down and honor your body's knowledge without feeling guilty or ashamed. While you may wait for approval from someone else, the only permission you need is your own. It's OK to live and work with greater ease, joy, and space; it's necessary to flourish. Each time you reconnect with and honor your body, you choose a new attitude and belief about work, relaxation, and your feeling of self-worth – you are actively rewriting your brain. When you reconnect with your body, you open the door to more insight, pleasure, joy, and a more easeful life.

Some Ways to Reconnect with Your Body

Our body and intellect are two halves of the same whole. Our minds pilot the ship while our bodies propel us onward. When we are overworked or emotionally stressed, our mind drifts away, leaving our body in a shell to fend for itself. Whether a short pick-me-up or a full-fledged exercise, moving the body brings the mind back to the present moment and a tendency for clarity, focus, and energy. Here are some ideas for getting back on the horse and reconnecting with your body:

Do Yoga

This is self-evident, yet there is always room for fresh discoveries. Aside from class, what does your body require today? Abby Tucker recommends taking your daily vitamins - 5 postures that your body requires every day to wake up, focus, and revive. Flow into the places that need some attention today, stretch into the pockets that are a little tight, and breathe into the spaces that want a little more heat. Stir the pot and listen to your body.[64]

---

[64] "Self-care - Wikipedia." https://en.wikipedia.org/wiki/Self-care.

Jump in a Cold Shower

Before you leave, please hear me out. Do you remember how nice it feels to spray cold water on your face? Try it on your whole body. Alternatively, you might begin warm and end chilly. A cold shower's therapeutic benefits include a surge of new blood throughout the body. The aftereffects include increased bodily awareness, a metabolic surge, and razor-sharp focus. For 60 seconds, try it! Alternatives include going for a swim or surfing on some winter swells.

Sing

Play your favorite music loudly, close your eyes, and sing like there is no tomorrow! Take in the vibration, your emotions, and the energy of your voice. Do you require some privacy? Try going to the restroom, showering, or getting in the car. The blossoming voice expands the body and the heart!

Grab a Snack

According to research, crisp and sour meals keep us awake. Follow the texture, listen for the crunch, relish the juiciness, and let the sweet and salty meet in your mouth while you munch. What remains? What pervades your eating experience? Allow your body to nurture you by immersing yourself in your experiences. Balancing has a fascinating way of cutting through the clutter and transporting you to the present moment. Enter the tree posture. Perform a fast headstand. Choose a position and focus your attention on the point of contact with the ground. Play with your weight, paying attention to where you're stiffening and where you may soften and relax. Longer holds allow the body to tune in and adjust, but more difficult positions need quick pin-point attention.

Hold Your Breath

"Take a deep breath; it'll make you feel better," we heard. Sure, but what about the other part of holding your breath? Working through a few rounds of breath retention, which boosts oxygen intake and engages the entire spectrum of our respiratory system, is one of my favorite ways to reconnect with my body. Begin with a complete inhalation on a count of four. Allow the air to enter your chest and fill your abdomen. Hold the breath for 8 counts at the peak of the inhale. Allow any 'holding' tension in the neck and jaws to ease. Exhale with a tiny constraint and let the breath release on a count of 8. 6-10 rounds should be enough. Allow prana to flow freely throughout your body.[65]

Walk Barefoot

Take your socks off and go for a walk. Ascend the steps. Play on the floor. Feel the deck's exposed timber. Extend your exploration and experience the moisture of the grass and the warmth of the concrete. Consider the bottoms of your feet — your kneels, arches, and small toes as they turn and move. Allow your feet to come to life and explore.

Dance N' Groove

Bring out the drums and crank up the music! Dancing is one of the most primitive techniques to arouse the body. Close your eyes, close

---

[65] "Why is Self-Care Important? - SNHU." 14 Apr. 2020, https://www.snhu.edu/about-us/newsroom/health/what-is-self-care.

your thoughts, and FEEL. Close your eyes and pay attention. Allow the music to grab your attention and move your impulses. Discover the fluidity of your joints and the weight of your bones, then let your body swirl, shake, and flow. Alternatives: find a partner and organize a dancing party!

Run for the Hills

For me, trail running combines two elements of magic: the ability to be in nature and terrain uncertainty. Call it a fight or flight response, or perhaps simply deeply entrenched muscle memory, but our bodies have an incredible ability to react in a moving environment. Set your speed on the trails and sharpen your senses. Allow your body to experience the action of a swift turn, a rapid drop, or the transition from soft dirt to hard rocks. Connect with your body and let your legs liberate you.

Get a Massage

Give yourself a massage; a little love and care for the body is a guaranteed way to reconnect. If it isn't an option right now, show yourself some love. Begin with the skull and work your fingertips across the whole scalp. Glide your hands from head to toe using long, forceful strokes. Grip and release the major muscular groups initially, then on to more sensitive places such as the neck and foot. When you're through, pause to let it all sink in. Welcome back, body... welcome back.

CHAPTER 4

Positive Self-Talk

Positive self-talk is an internal conversation that makes people feel good about themselves. Positive self-talk may help a person think positively and feel inspired. Recognizing negative self-talk is the first step toward more optimistic thinking. Self-talk or internal conversation refers to a person's communication with oneself. It is an organic cognitive process. When confronted with barriers or problems, people may engage in greater self-talk. People employ self-talk either silently or aloud to themselves. Positive or negative self-talk is possible. This book addresses the benefits of positive self-talk. It also shows how people can quit the practice of negative self-talk.

According to clinical and forensic neuropsychologist Judy Ho, Ph.D., positive self-talk is about speaking to oneself and treating yourself with care and compassion, just as you treat someone you love. It is influenced by positive psychology, which she defines as "the study of what causes individuals to thrive and function optimally. It's about concentrating on our strengths rather than our flaws and leveraging our skills to address difficulties in our life."

Despite its benefits, positive self-talk is sometimes confused with "toxic positivity," or the inclination to suppress bad emotions to maintain a "good vibes only" attitude. Positive self-talk, on the other hand, is not harmful. Optimistic self-talk, according to Whitney Goodman, LMFT, a licensed psychotherapist located in Miami, Florida, is not about being constantly positive because let's be honest, that's not feasible or good. Instead, Goodman says that positive self-talk takes a more neutral approach as a method of understanding and responding to your ideas and feelings.[66]

"It doesn't imply we'll always feel wonderful when we employ [positive self-talk], or it'll be simple to access," adds Goodman. "It's quite difficult at times. Some conditions are simply unfavorable." If reciting all of the affirmations doesn't work for you, consider positive self-talk as a practical and empowered way of thinking rather than continual positivism. Perspective is also important in positive self-talk. Positive self-talk, according to Kevin Gilliland, PsyD, a licensed clinical psychologist and executive director of Innovation360, an outpatient counseling program, is a talent that develops as you get a better grasp of and respect for perspective. You may detect hope and optimism in a circumstance. "When people battle with melancholy, anxiety, or any other psychological condition, we tend to acquire a negative bias, seeing the impossible and the bad while ignoring encouraging or hopeful things," Dr. Gilliland explains. "When we

---

[66] "Self Care." https://selfcare.time.com.my/auth/login.

have a larger, more balanced, or fair view of the problem, we can perceive alternative, non-negative options."

The Connection between Mental and Physical Health

We can't address mental health without also talking about physical health. The two are linked and affect one another. "If something occurs to you physically, you will have some mental symptoms associated with that shift," says Goodman. "You will almost certainly make up a tale about what is occurring to you physically. You will interpret the symptoms and indicators. Likewise, certain emotions may arise due to the bodily changes or experiences you are encountering."[67]

According to Goodman, persons with physical diseases are more likely to acquire mental health difficulties such as sadness and anxiety as a symptom or the stress of treating the physical ailment. Likewise, vice versa: According to Dr. Gilliland, it is also typical for persons suffering from mental illnesses to experience physical symptoms such as irritable bowel syndrome or sleep disorders. "I think that's excellent news because we have a lot of alternatives, other than therapy and pharmaceuticals, to assist manage our psychological health," he adds.[68]

---

[67] "Self-Talk | Psychology Today." https://www.psychologytoday.com/us/basics/self-talk.
[68] "Self-Talk: Why It Matters - Healthline." 12 Jul. 2016, https://www.healthline.com/health/mental-health/self-talk.

Implementing Positive Self-Talk in Your Daily Routine
Ensure The Positive Self-Talk Feels True

When you're feeling bad and psychologically down, Goodman says positive affirmations can sound forced, inauthentic, and like outright falsehoods, making them less effective. Assume that your positive affirmation is to appreciate your body every day. That sounds fantastic, but there will be moments when you just do not. It might be challenging to incorporate positive affirmation on days when you glance in the mirror, and negative ideas take control. Instead, Goodman suggests coming up with a more dynamic phrase that doesn't appear forced or artificial. There is no universal endorsement. So, experiment with words until you find ones that speak to you.

Change Your Behavior

Saying or believing a positive notion is one thing, but following through with new action is what truly transforms. "If you continue to participate in activities that refute or are utterly antithetical to this notion, integrating the positive affirmation will become much more difficult," Goodman explains. Using positive self-talk alone is essentially the same as talking the talk but not doing the walk. Goodman suggests making it a habit to ask oneself, "How can I act out this affirmation?" Or, how can I put my affirmation into action? For instance, if your affirmation is to focus on loving your body, what everyday acts would you do to convey that love to your body?[69][70]

Start With Positive Self-Talk in One Area

If you've ever attempted to start a new habit, you know that change is difficult. And, no matter how ambitious you are, attempting to alter too many things at once is typically a formula for disaster. Instead of trying a comprehensive makeover of your self-talk all at once, Goodman recommends concentrating on one aspect of your life when you'd like to enhance your self-talk, such as self-love, health, wellbeing, or confidence. Begin with the area where you are the harshest on yourself, then consider how you want to feel about that area and create positive affirmations based on your aspirations. Remember to keep it realistic and honest so that you can put your energy and thoughts behind it. Positive self-talk, like other good practices, gains momentum. So, once you're on a roll with positive self-talk in one area, Goodman says, it'll be simpler to include it in others.

Collect All the Data Without Judgment

Another technique to practice positive self-talk is to develop the habit of gathering all relevant information about a situation before passing judgment. "When we are going through a tough situation, we tend to be biased towards what isn't functioning, broken, or we can't accomplish," explains Dr. Gilliland. So, by gathering all of the data, not just the negative bits, you have a more balanced picture

---

[69] "Positive Self-Talk: Benefits and Techniques - Healthline." 17 Oct. 2018, https://www.healthline.com/health/positive-self-talk.
[70] "What is Positive Self-Talk? (Incl. Examples)." 21 Sept. 2021, https://positivepsychology.com/positive-self-talk/.

and can evaluate what is genuinely functioning, what isn't wrong, or what action steps you can take. Of course, Dr. Gilliland continues, this will not change the issue, but changing your viewpoint on it may make a big difference in how you feel and handle it.

Question Your Thoughts

Although they may feel accurate, keep in mind that thoughts are not always facts. When a negative idea arises, Dr. Ho suggests asking yourself if it is comprehensive, accurate, and balanced. "If you say no to any of that, this notion may need to be retooled," she adds. "It's all about accepting that ideas are nothing more than mental happenings. Just because you have an idea doesn't guarantee it's true." Dr. Ho recommends adopting the "yes, but" strategy to develop a more comprehensive, accurate, and balanced perspective. So, you'd say, "Yes, I haven't finished this large job yet, but I've made a lot of progress, and I'm ready to keep going." Or, "Yes, 2020 was a bad performance, but I also had a lot of alone time that allowed me to focus on my health."

Work With a Professional

Finally, if you're having trouble incorporating positive self-talk, seek the advice of a professional, such as a therapist or psychologist. "Negative self-talk may sometimes be so profound that it is a substantial factor in a person's clinical depression or anxiety," Dr. Ho explains. That's when you'll need the support of an expert who can help you go even farther and deeper into some of these strategies. Dr. Gilliland says you may discover aspects of your situation that you hadn't previously considered because of your anxiety or depression when dealing with a professional.

What are the Benefits of Positive Self-Talk?

Positive self-talk has improved mental health, performance, and relationships. 2020 Iranian research, for example, revealed that self-talk influenced how individuals coped with anxiety during the COVID-19 epidemic. In addition, positive self-talkers reported less fear about dying and fewer symptoms of obsessive-compulsive disorder (OCD). The study also discovered that persons who used positive self-talk acquired excellent coping techniques for their emotions and mental stress.[71][72]

According to a 2019 study, students who uttered a self-affirming statement before giving a speech or presentation reported less performance anxiety than those who did not. Positive self-talk may motivate and benefit athletes and those who participate in sports. 2020 investigation According to Trusted Source, positive self-talk can also assist athletes in staying motivated and having fun. According to research, how people address themselves during self-talk influences their feelings. According to a 2014 review by trusted Source, using non-first-person pronouns such as 'you' and one's name instead of first-person pronouns such as 'I' helps people control their thoughts, feelings, and actions under social stress. This notion is supported by a 2019 study, which found that utilizing second-person pronouns in positive self-talk enhanced performance times and output in endurance sports conditions.

---

[71] "What Is Self-Talk - Think Affirmations." 05 Jan. 2021, https://thinkaffirmations.com/self-talk/.
[72] "15 Ways to Practice Positive Self-Talk for Success - Lifehack." https://www.lifehack.org/504756/self-talk-determines-your-success-15-tips.

What Impact Does Negative Self-Talk Have?

When people are uncomfortable or uncertain or lack confidence or self-belief, they may indulge in negative self-talk. Negative self-talk may harm a person's self-esteem and conviction in their worth and talents. According to the College of Cognitive Behavioural Therapies (CCBT), negative self-talk can create a vicious cycle and a self-fulfilling prophecy. For example, if a person tells himself that they will be unable to complete a task, they are less likely to put out the necessary effort. When they fail, the individual may think, "I knew I couldn't do it." That's not unusual." Individuals can employ positive self-talk to fight negative thought patterns (RNT). According to recent research, RNT is a risk factor for the intensity, duration, and relapse of depression and anxiety.[73][74]

Recognizing negative self-talk and changing it before it takes hold can assist people in thinking more positively and changing their behavior. According to the CCBT, positive or negative self-talk becomes a habit that people may modify. The first step in improving one's self-talk is to recognize negative thoughts. When dealing with adversity, one should pay attention to how one speaks to oneself. It may be beneficial to record examples of negative self-talk. People might then consider other useful things to say to themselves in difficult times.

If a person's mental health is being harmed by negative self-talk, they should consult a doctor. Negative self-talk and recurrent thoughts may indicate the presence of an underlying disease such

---

[73] "Mindfulness & Meditation - Harvard University." https://www.harvard.edu/in-focus/mindfulness-meditation/.

[74] "Meditation for Beginners: 20 Practical Tips for ... - zen habits." https://zenhabits.net/meditation-guide/.

as anxiety, depression, or OCD. A doctor may refer a patient to support groups or health experts who can assist them in dealing with negative self-talk. Making lifestyle modifications may occasionally assist someone who has negative thinking patterns or self-talk. According to research by trusted Sources, exercising can help alleviate anxiety. Mindfulness and meditation are two activities that can help a person feel more pleasant and calm.

Self-talk is a natural cognitive process that involves an individual's internal discourse with themselves. Positive self-talk may make you feel more encouraged, driven, and hopeful. When faced with adversity, it can be employed as a coping method. Positive affirmations and self-talk can help people overcome negative thinking and boost their confidence and self-esteem. However, if a person has recurring negative thoughts or self-talk, they should see a doctor since they may have an underlying mental health disorder.

The Power of Positive Self-Talk

Before proceeding, it should be stated that positive self-talk does not imply disregarding life's bad or unpleasant parts. Instead, it's about changing the narrative to positively and constructively handle these difficulties. For example, if you commit a mistake at work, it may provoke a memory of being punished for the fault. "I can't believe I did that!" you exclaim inside. I'm such a moron, and I'll pay for it afterward!" Instead, remind yourself, "Tomorrow is another chance to try again, using the lessons from today." When used regularly, positive self-talk has the potential to:

- Increase your happiness.
- Reduce anxiety and stress

- Promotes healthy behaviors
- Reduce negative emotions and psychological symptoms
- Encourage self-assurance

Consequently, your psychological and physical well-being, coping abilities, and life span may improve. You could even see improvements in your immune system, personal relationships, or job performance.

Even if you believe you just have a limited amount of time, spend a few minutes each day doing something for yourself. It's not self-centered. Instead, it engages in activities that revitalize your general and health-related well-being. Mindfulness meditation, physical activities, cooking nutritious meals, and doing things that make you joyful, such as playing with your children or reading a book outside, are self-care. Of course, you can't just stick your head in the sand. You can, however, reduce the amount of negativity in your life. For example, to avoid "room scrolling," you might delete social networking applications from your phone. If you have a toxic buddy, you may want to limit your time with them and instead surround yourself with more positive individuals.[75][76]

Finding the things, you're grateful for may improve your mood, whether you keep a gratitude diary or just have a mental checklist. This will gradually lead to better self-talk since you'll be focused on what you have rather than what you don't. Have you found yourself saying "I can't" too frequently? If this is the case, you are reducing

---

[75] "4 Common Types of Self-Talk - Mindful." 12 Sept. 2016, https://www.mindful.org/4-common-types-self-talk/.

[76] "Positive thinking: Reduce stress by eliminating negative self-talk ...." 03 Feb. 2022, https://www.mayoclinic.org/healthy-lifestyle/stress-management/in-depth/positive-thinking/art-20043950.

your chances of success. Take this term out of your lexicon and replace it with "I can."

Stop what you're doing and check in with your feelings if you see a negative idea coming in. You don't have to come to a complete halt right now. Instead, when you have the opportunity, remove yourself from the situation, cool down, and consider ways to put a positive perspective on the problem. You may also shift your perspective by carefully posting positive affirmations and mantras throughout your house and office to serve as visual reminders to be happy and caring.

Laughter is, without a doubt, the finest medicine. So, go ahead and laugh at yourself. Whether it's watching a YouTube video, remembering a hilarious former encounter, or spending time with someone who constantly makes you grin. Finally, if you've done everything else and still haven't changed how you talk to yourself, it's time to see a mental health expert. They can help you identify the sources of your self-talk and devise tactics for changing the script.

Your self-talk may be damaging your stress levels without your knowledge! Self-talk—the way your inner voice interprets the world around you and communicates with your inner self—can significantly impact your stress levels in various ways. For example, suppose you usually have negative self-talk. In that case, you may be interpreting situations in your life as more stressful than they need to be, causing yourself undue anxiety and tension. You may also fall into rumination, a negative thought habit that may fill your free time and bring the past into the present unnecessarily without resolution.[77][78][79]

---

[77] "What is Meditation - Headspace." https://www.headspace.com/meditation-101/what-is-meditation.
[78] "What Does Meditation Mean? Meditation Definition (And Why It Matters)." https://mindworks.org/blog/meditation-definition/.
[79] "Beginners Guide to Meditation: Techniques & Tips to Learn to Sit [Video]." https://mindworks.org/blog/beginners-guide-meditation/.

CHAPTER 5

Meditation for Self-Love

It's all too easy to become engrossed in negative thoughts and self-doubt. Underneath those sentiments of inadequacy and fear is frequently a deeper truth: we do not believe we are deserving of love. Societal norms teach us to strive to be "better continually." That implies you'll be slimmer, happier, richer, wiser, etc. We are rarely taught that we are sufficient simply as we are. It is awful if we do not believe we are deserving of our love. My yogic sensibility tells me to halt, relax, and breathe when my inner critic convinces me that I'll never be successful or happy. I sometimes grab for the ice cream instead and opt to wallow. The rabbit hole of negativity continues, though, and the recovery period is usually lengthier. Mastering the variety of human emotions daily may be quite difficult. I've discovered that when I lapse into "not-enoughness," that's when I need to focus on loving myself the most.

Consider attempting meditation if stress makes you nervous, tense, and concerned. This procedure may improve both physical and mental well-being. Meditation may provide you with a sense of quiet, tranquility, and balance, enhancing your emotional well-being and general health. You may also utilize it to relieve tension and relax by concentrating your attention on something relaxing. Meditation can help you learn to stay balanced and at peace within yourself. These advantages do not cease when your meditation practice does. Meditation can help you navigate your day more calmly. Meditation may also aid in the management of symptoms associated with certain medical illnesses.[80][81]

Don't allow the concept of meditating "properly" to add to your anxiety. You can attend specific meditation centers or group programs guided by certified instructors if you so choose. However, you may easily practice meditation on your own. You might also discover applications to utilize. You may also make meditation as official or informal as you like, depending on your lifestyle and environment. They may, for example, begin and conclude each day with an hour of meditation. But all you need is a few minutes of uninterrupted meditation time.

Stepping into Self-Love

There are several methods to care for ourselves and demonstrate self-love. We can read uplifting poetry, get a massage, go on long

---

[80] "Change Your Self-Talk | Psychology Today." 05 Nov. 2019, https://www.psychologytoday.com/us/blog/loving-through-your-differences/201911/change-your-self-talk.
[81] "Negative Self Talk: What It Is and Strategies to Stop It." https://mantracare.org/therapy/self-care/negative-self-talk/.

walks in nature, or seek help from a friend (or therapist). We can also turn to our practice as yogis. I've found that focusing on self-love helps me reconnect with my heart—to remember that I am deserving of love, especially my own. When I meditate on self-love, I can be completely open and honest. It's an act of love to sit with my thoughts and feelings rather than attempting to push them away. When I meditate with my heart in mind, I can create a loving place where I may feel whatever I need to feel without judgment. I'm not beating myself up over anything I believe I did wrong or how I didn't "measure up" during this time. I'm just letting myself be human.

I can feel myself falling away from the feeling of this compassionate place as soon as I leave the present moment and allow my thoughts to absorb my attention. Meditation teaches me that ideas are transient; they come and go. When I take a step back and let them pass, I realize that whatever inadequacy I feel is only fleeting. Use this meditation to help remind yourself that you are worthy of your love and compassion when experiencing feelings of self-doubt and low self-esteem.

Begin by making yourself comfortable. You can either sit on a bolster or a few folded blankets while lying on your back with a bolster under your knees and a folded blanket behind your head. Next, allow yourself to be supported by a chair or sit against a wall.

Feel the connection between your back and the mat if you're lying down. If you're sitting, stretch your spine, expand your collarbones, and put your hands on your thighs (palms facing either up or down). Once you're comfortable, close your eyes or lessen your sight and focus on your breathing. Take note of your breathing without attempting to alter it. Also, note whether you are tight or relaxed without attempting to modify either.

Exhale via your mouth after inhaling through your nose. Continue to breathe deeply and fully through your nose and your mouth. As you breathe, pay attention to your body and the state of your thoughts. What parts of your body are tense? Do you feel emotionally walled off or shut down? What happened to your mind? Is it straying, or is it at ease inside the breath? Is your mind calm or riddled with agitation, negativity, and uncertainty?[82][83]

Continue to inhale through your nose and exhale through your mouth while placing both hands over your heart. Consider how it feels to lay your hands over this soft spot, this place where you feel love for yourself and others. Allow your breath to become smoother and easier, and then begin to breathe in and out via your nose. Feel the passage of air entering your lungs and then out into the world. Imagine that you are releasing any bad ideas that may be remaining in your head with each breath.

Continue to concentrate on your breathing. Think "I am worthy" on each inhalation and "I am enough" on each exhalation. Allow each inhalation to bring self-love and exhalation to release what no longer serves you. Take a few moments to breathe and repeat this mantra to yourself. Take note of how you feel when you repeat these sentences to yourself. It's acceptable if your thoughts wander at any moment. It is human nature for the mind to wander. Simply return your attention to your breathing. Observe how your pleasant or negative ideas arrive and go, and simply let them pass by like clouds in the sky.

---

[82] "Listening to self-talk for 15 minutes a day can change your life.."
https://www.selftalkplus.com/.
[83] "The Power of Positive Self Talk (and How You Can Use It)." 09 Jun. 2021,
https://www.betterup.com/blog/self-talk.

Now imagine yourself in front of a mirror, looking into your own eyes. What do you notice? Sadness and pain? Love and happiness? Neutrality? Whatever you see in the mirror, tell yourself, "I love you," "you are lovely," and "you are worthy of happiness." Be aware that what you see in the mirror right now may alter from what you see the next time you look.

Consider breathing into your heart and visualizing love pouring out of your hands and into your heart. Allow this love to warm and saturate you from the center of your heart, filling the rest of your body. Feel peace and serenity move up through your chest, neck, and head, into your shoulders, arms, and hands, and down into your ribs, belly, pelvis, legs, and feet. Allow a warm sensation to fill you from head to toe. Breathe in this space and know that love is always there for you when you need it.

Take a few more deep, thoughtful breaths, and then gently open your eyes when you're ready. Sit for a few moments to reflect on your one-of-a-kind meditation experience. When you need to create a loving space for yourself, return to this practice or any other resource you have. This is a wonderful opportunity to discover something new about yourself and become more aware of your bodily and mental needs. Allow self-love to help you create a deeper relationship with yourself and show up more fully in your life.[84][85]

As the speed of our existence quickens, fueled by a slew of causes apparently beyond our control, an increasing number of us are drawn to meditation, to this radical act of being. We are moving

---

[84] "How to Do Positive Self-Talk - The Wellness Society | Self-Help ...."
https://thewellnesssociety.org/positive-self-talk/.

[85] "Self-Talk Plus+ on the App Store." 03 May. 2021,
https://apps.apple.com/us/app/self-talk-plus/id1562158353.

toward contemplative awareness for various reasons, not the least of which is to retain our individual and communal sanity, regain our perspective and sense of meaning, or simply cope with our day's unprecedented stress and uncertainty.

We discover this by intentionally stopping and falling awake to how things are in this moment, without succumbing to our reactions and judgments, by working wisely with such occurrences with a healthy dose of self-compassion when we succumb, and by our willingness to take up residence in the present moment despite all our plans and activities aimed at getting somewhere else, completing a project, or pursuing desired objects or goals. Simply sitting down and being alone for a while is a radical gesture of love.[86][87]

Loving-kindness, compassion, sympathetic joy, and serenity are all difficult meditation techniques used to create one-pointed focused attention, from which the powers of these invoked characteristics arise, transfiguring the heart. Simply recognizing these heart traits and emphasizing their relevance in our practice may help us recognize them when they occur spontaneously during mindfulness practice. In addition, especially during tough times, orient the heart and thoughts in that direction more regularly.

These practices, particularly loving-kindness, may frequently serve as a necessary and helpful antidote to mental states such as furious fury, which may be too intense to respond to via direct observation unless one's practice is extremely developed. Formal loving-kindness practice can help soften one's relationship to such

---

[86] "How To Meditate - Meditation 101: Meditation Techniques & Benefits ...." https://www.gaiam.com/blogs/discover/meditation-101-techniques-benefits-and-a-beginner-s-how-to.

[87] "Sahaja Yoga Meditation." https://www.singaporemeditation.org/.

enormously afflictive mental states, allowing us to avoid succumbing to their forces. In addition, it makes them more accessible and less difficult to deal with.

However, with practice, direct observation becomes the incarnation of loving-kindness and compassion in and of itself. It can accept any thought state, no matter how afflictive or poisonous. And in seeing and understanding it—in open-hearted, nonjudgmental presence—we may look into the nature of the rage or sadness for whatever it is. And, as we have seen, it attenuates, diminishes, and vanishes when we see it, embrace it, and know it, much like touching a soap bubble or writing on water. What develops in such moments is nothing less than loving-kindness itself, which arises organically from lengthy quiet, without any invitation since it is always present.

Meditation for deep self-and-other-healing

Bring your consciousness to the breath and the body as a whole in a dignified sitting position or lying down, whichever you like. Breathe and rest here, developing a relatively solid foundation of moment-to-moment awareness while you ride the breath's waves.

Imagine someone in your life who loves you or has unconditionally loved you when you feel comfortable relaxing with the rhythm of your breathing. Evoking and surrendering to the qualities of their unselfish love and compassion, as well as the entire aura or field of their love for you—right here, right now, breathing with these sensations, soaking in them, resting in the warmth and light of their passionate embrace of you exactly as you are. Or reveling in the knowledge that you are totally and unambiguously loved and accepted just as you are—without having to be different, without being worthy of their affection, and not being particularly deserving.

You might not feel especially worthy or deserved. That is irrelevant. It is, in reality, unimportant. The important thing to remember is that you were or are loved. They adore you just as you are. You have always been for who you are now and maybe always will be. Allowing your heart to luxuriate in these sensations, cradled in them, and become entangled in them. To be shaken moment by moment by the swinging rhythmic pounding of another's loving heart. Inhaling and exhaling in rhythm with your breath, allowing the warmth of this pulsating field of loving-kindness to embrace and bathe your heart.[88][89]

If you're having trouble recalling or conjuring up such a person from memory right now, try imagining someone treating you in that manner. And envision the sensations of love, compassion, and regard with remarkable vividness. And it can be equally useful in this practice. Then, when you're ready, check if you can become both the cause and the object of these identical sensations. In other words, adopt these sentiments as if they were your own rather than those of another. Lingering as long as you can with your own heart's regular pounding. Carrying in your heart sentiments of love, acceptance, and kindness for oneself, free of any judgment. Just bathing in sentiments of loving-kindness is analogous to a mother's all-loving hug for her kid—where you are both the mother and the child simultaneously. Resting as much as you can in these

---

[88] "Self-talk - what is it and why is it important? | healthdirect."
https://www.healthdirect.gov.au/self-talk.
[89] "Positive self-talk: Benefits, examples, and tips." 18 Mar. 2022,
https://www.medicalnewstoday.com/articles/positive-self-talk.

sensations from moment to moment. I'm bathing in your honor. Your unconditional acceptance of yourself as you are right now. Allowing this experience to be self-sufficient and natural, rather than pushed or compelled.

While resting in this field of loving-kindness, this embrace of loving-kindness, you may find it helpful to whisper to yourself or hear them whispered to you by the wind, the air, your breath, the world, or even asserted more strongly with great feeling, the following phrases: May I be pleased and joyful? May I be well and whole to the greatest extent possible? May I have a sense of well-being?

Gently repeat, at your speed, internally whispering, inwardly listening, feeling, knowing, affirming: May I be secure, protected, and free from inner and outward harm. May I be pleased and joyful? May I be well and whole to the greatest extent possible? May I have a sense of well-being? May I be secure, protected, and free from internal and external damage? May I be pleased and joyful? May I be well and whole to the greatest extent possible? May I have a sense of well-being?

It may feel strange at first to be speaking or even thinking such things to oneself. After all, who is this "I" hoping for this? And who is the "I" who is the recipient of these wishes? Nevertheless, both eventually fade into the experience of being secure and free from danger now, comfortable and joyful at this time, and complete because you are already entire. The sensation of resting in the comfort of well-being, apart from the dis-ease and fragmentation we frequently experience. This sensation, this sensation, is the core of loving-kindness.

However, you may object. Why am I concentrating on myself if this is a selfless practice? On my sense of security and well-being? On my contentment? One argument might be that you are not distinct from the cosmos that gave birth to you and hence are as deserving of loving-kindness as everything or anybody else. Your loving-kindness cannot be both loving and kind if it excludes oneself. However, you should not be concerned. It's not just about you. Because the realm of loving-kindness is infinite, if you choose, you might think of the loving-kindness practice as we've been doing it up to this point as tuning your instrument before you perform it in public. In this scenario, tuning the instrument is a big act of love and kindness in and of itself, not a means to a goal.[90][91]

After you've formed a reasonably steady field of loving-kindness around yourself and remained in the sensation of being held, cradled, and rocked in its embrace, you can actively extend the field of the heart, exactly as we sometimes do in mindfulness practice. For example, we may extend the sphere of loving-kindness around our hearts and ask other creatures to join us, either individually or collectively. Unfortunately, this is not always so simple. As a result, it's best to be one person for whom you naturally feel loving-kindness, and only if you're willing to explore it. Otherwise, simply continue to embrace yourself as the receiver of your love and compassion, utilizing the terms we've previously used or adapting them to fit yourself.

---

[90] "SELF-TALK - Winona State University." 29 Nov. 2016, https://www.winona.edu/resilience/Media/Self-Talk-Worksheet.pdf.
[91] "Self-Talk Scripts: List Of Positive Affirmations [500+]." 31 Jan. 2019, https://mindbodypal.com/self-talk-scripts/.

So, if you are willing to extend the field of loving-kindness beyond your own heart, body, and existence, in your mind's eye and heart, conjuring, for now, the sensation or picture of a human, a person for whom you have a tremendous fondness, someone you were emotionally close to. Can you cherish this person in your heart with the same loving-kindness you have shown to yourself? Whether it's a kid or a father, a brother or a sister, a grandmother or other close or distant family, a close friend or a treasured neighbor, alone or together. Breathe in your heart with them, him, or her. Keep them close to your heart. As best you can imagine them in your heart. Because, so that you know, this technique is so strong on its own that no amount of vivid imagery of yourself or others is required for it to be extremely successful. And best wishes: May she, he, and they be secure, protected, and free from inner and outside harm. May she, he, and they all be happy. May she, he, and they be as healthy and whole as possible. May she, he, and they all feel at peace.

Moment by moment, linger in your own heart's field of loving-kindness. With these sentences as you silently repeat them to yourself, and much more so with the emotion behind them. Repeating them in order, not mechanically, not like a mantra, but thoughtfully, completely aware of what you're saying. Feeling the intention behind the intention and the intention and feeling behind each statement. May she, he, and they are secure and protected from internal and external danger. May she, he, and they all be happy. May she, he, or they are as healthy and whole as possible. May she, he, or they enjoy a sense of well-being.

If your mind wanders or you are suffering at a given time, simply notice what is going on in your head. Perhaps you are having difficulty keeping your attention or concentration. And simply, include yourself in the field of loving-kindness repeatedly, returning to the sentences murmured, said inwardly to yourself, resting in the emotion radiating out of those syllables, and underneath that, out of your heart. Moment by moment, with whomever you're sending loving-kindness, singularly or collectively.

And, if you like, you can now broaden your range of awareness to include one or more people who are truly troublesome for you in some manner, perhaps because you share a terrible background. Who may have injured you and whom you regard as more of an enemy or an impediment than a friend? This does not imply that you are being asked to forgive someone for everything they may have done to injure you or others. You merely acknowledge that they are human beings with ambitions and, most likely, a desire to be happy and secure.

Then, to the best of your abilities — and only to the degree that you're ready to do it — extend loving-kindness to them as well, for all the difficulties and issues that lay between you: May she, he, or they be safe and protected from all kinds of harm, both within and outside. May she, he, or they are comfortable and happy. May she, he, or they are as healthy and whole as possible. May she, he, or they enjoy a sense of well-being.

It's like mindfulness meditation, where we may focus on a single object of attention or widen our focus to cover a wider range of possibilities. These options are equally legitimate and healing, and they all ultimately lead to each other.

So, suppose you want to cultivate loving-kindness simply toward yourself now, in this moment of practice. That is acceptable, and you can just retain and sustain that dimension of the loving-kindness practice beneath my voice and what I'm saying. Likewise, if you choose to direct loving-kindness toward individuals you know and love, or even just one person, that is perfectly OK. Any degree to which you choose to grow and direct loving-kindness is acceptable, even ideal. And, in the end, embodies all of the others. Since you may feel yourself naturally driven to bring more and more creatures into the sphere of loving-kindness emanating from your own heart and being in all ways, both inside and externally, over time, or you may discover that they appear unexpectedly at times. It's worth noting this. How come they show up if you aren't intentionally inviting them in? And how do they get in? Hmmm... Perhaps your heart is bigger and smarter than you realize.

In the spirit of the heart's boundlessness and love itself, we may broaden the field of loving-kindness to embrace our neighbors and neighborhood, our community, our state, our nation, and, if you wish, the entire globe. Your pets, all animal life, all life, all plant life, the entire ecosystem, and all sentient beings may all be included. You may even be quite particular and include individual persons, especially political leaders, in your loving-kindness field. As difficult as it may be if you vehemently disagree with them and find yourself severely condemning them and even their fundamental humanity. Even more, the incentive to include them. They are worthy of loving-kindness because they are human, and they may respond by softening in ways your intellect cannot fathom. And possibly the same is true for you.[92][93]

---

[92] "Parker Jack – Self Talk Lyrics | Genius Lyrics." 11 Mar. 2022, https://genius.com/Parker-jack-self-talk-lyrics.
[93] "Self-Talk - InsideEWU." https://inside.ewu.edu/calelearning/psychological-skills/self-talk/.

You may also include individuals less fortunate than yourself who are exploited at work or home in your area of loving-kindness. Everyone is imprisoned, whether rightfully or unjustly. Those who are at the mercy of their adversaries. Everyone who is hospitalized, ill, or dying. All those caught up in chaos, living in terror, and suffering in any shape or form. Yet, whatever has brought them to this point in their life, they, like us, desire to experience the ease of well-being rather than dis-ease and fragmentation. They are all seeking happiness and contentment. They are all striving to be entire and healthy. They all want to be secure and undamaged.

So, we acknowledge this method in which we are all connected in our desire to be happy and not suffer, and we wish them well: May all beings, both near and distant, be secure, protected, and free of inner and exterior harm. May all beings, near and distant, be pleased and joyful. May all beings, near and distant, be as healthy and whole as possible. May all beings, near and distant, have peace and happiness. May all beings, both near and distant, be secure, protected, and free of inner and exterior harm. May all beings, near and distant, be pleased and joyful. May all beings, near and distant, be as healthy and whole as possible. And all beings, near and distant, have a sense of well-being.

And it doesn't have to end there. Why not include the entire planet in the loving-kindness field? Why not embrace the earth that we call home? That is an organism in its own right. This body can be thrown off balance by her actions, conscious and unconscious, in ways that pose huge threats to the life it nurtures and the intelligence embedded within all aspects of that life, animal, plant, and mineral that interacts so seamlessly in the natural world. So, we may broaden the scope of our loving-kindness even further by expanding the field of the loving heart.

Once again, embrace the entire planet and the entire cosmos in which our Earth is simply an atom, and we are not even a quark. May our planet and the entire cosmos be secure and free of inner and outside damage. May our planet and the entire cosmos be pleased and joyful. May this planet and the universe be entire and healthy. May our planet and the entire universe feel happiness. May our planet and the entire cosmos be secure and free of inner and outside damage. May our planet and the entire cosmos be pleased and joyful. Make our world and the entire universe healthy and whole. May our planet and the entire universe feel happiness.

So, in the dying minutes of our time together, rest here in the brilliance and luminosity of your inner beauty, love, and compassion. Whether you use words or not, at whatever level you choose or are pulled to intuitively. Near and far, radiating loving-kindness within and outwardly. And, as this formal period of practicing together concludes with the sound of the bells, assert inside that this practice may be maintained regularly if you feel drawn to keep it alive and robust. As can all of the other activities we've been doing together, validating yourself and others, if you will, the old Navajo phrase, which I now offer to you: May you walk in beauty. May you, as well as all beings near and distant, wander in splendor.

CHAPTER 6

The Importance of Self-Love

To many people, self-love conjures up images of hippies and cheesy self-help books. However, it is important to practice self-compassion and self-love to maintain good mental health and prevent depression and anxiety. We'll look at some of the things you can do to cultivate this basic emotion in the sections below. "Why is self-love so important?" you may wonder. Unfortunately, self-love may appear to be a luxury rather than a necessity for many of us — or a new-age craze for individuals with too much free time.[94][95]

---

[94] "Self-Compassion." https://self-compassion.org/.
[95] "How to Practice Self-Compassion: 8 Techniques and Tips." 26 Oct. 2021, https://positivepsychology.com/how-to-practice-self-compassion/.

Ironically, those who work too hard and continually attempt to outdo themselves and grasp the shape-shifting phantom of perfection may require the most self-care and compassion. We are often too critical of ourselves because we want to achieve and do everything perfectly. This implies a lot of self-criticisms, and perfectionism is characterized by that persecutory inner voice that always reminds us how we could've done things better. Perfectionists are more likely to suffer from various ailments, both physical and mental, according to research, and self-compassion may help us break free. Perfectionism and self-compassion are, therefore, intricately intertwined. This book will look at strategies to reduce the former and increase the latter to believe that doing so would help you live a better, more fulfilled life.

The Ills of Perfectionism

Most of us were trained to think that perfectionism is a desirable trait in the Western world. After all, obsessing over flawless details leads to great work, and this personality trait allows us to humblebrag during job interviews. Perfectionism, on the other hand, is harmful to your health. Not merely "not optimal" or "harmful when overindulged," but detrimental. As in smoking or fat. A shortened lifespan, irritable bowel syndrome, fibromyalgia, eating disorders, depression, and suicide ideation are some of the negative health consequences associated with perfectionism. Recovering from heart illness or cancer is also more difficult for perfectionists, who are more prone to anxiety and sadness than the average population.

Moving Away from Perfectionism

So, how can we break free from perfectionism? First, recognize that it is harmful to you; beating yourself up over minor mistakes ultimately erodes your sense of self-worth and makes you unhappy. And you are entitled to better. In other words, happiness is something you are entitled to, not something you must work for. Even the United Nations recognized that the "pursuit of pleasure is a fundamental human objective." After years of training this inner bully, you acquire an unconscious tendency to put yourself down for every tiny thing, no matter how silly or nonsensical. From missing a deadline to spilling a teaspoon on the floor, perfectionists will continually criticize themselves for remote reasons — therefore, criticizing oneself for criticizing yourself is not unusual. Finally, you may begin to cultivate some much-needed self-compassion. You could believe that self-love is something you either have or don't have, but psychologists say that it is something you can develop.

What is Self-Compassion?

Compassion for oneself is fundamentally the same as compassion for others. Consider how it feels to be touched by kindness. To have compassion for others, you must first recognize their pain. For example, you can't feel sympathy for a homeless person on the street if you ignore them. Second, compassion is being affected by the suffering of others to the point where your heart responds to their agony (the word compassion means "to suffer with"). When this happens, you experience a sense of warmth and care and somehow want to assist the individual. Compassion also entails showing others tolerance and kindness when they fail or make errors, rather than passing harsh judgment.

Instead of dismissing your discomfort with a stiff upper lip, you pause to remind yourself, "This is truly tough right now... At this moment, how can I soothe and care for myself? Self-compassion implies you are compassionate and sympathetic when confronted with personal faults rather than relentlessly criticizing and blaming oneself for different deficiencies or weaknesses — after all, who ever said you were meant to be perfect? You may strive to change to be healthier and happier, but you do so because you care about yourself, not because you are useless or undesirable as you are. Perhaps most crucially, compassion for oneself implies that you recognize and embrace your humanity. Things do not always turn out the way you expect them to. You will experience disappointments, and losses, make blunders, run against your limits, and fall short of your goals. This is the human condition, a common reality for all of us. [96][97]

Have you ever gotten angry at...yourself? You blamed yourself and then beat yourself up for doing something you afterward regretted? Perhaps you've been harsh with someone just to be worse with yourself later? It's easy to be hard on yourself—we do it more than we know. But what if there was another option? Self-compassion is demonstrated when we forgive ourselves, accept our apparent imperfections, and offer ourselves, love. It is frequently much more difficult than it appears, but we may learn to make it a habit that

---

[96] "Self–Compassion - GoodTherapy." 17 Jun. 2019, https://www.goodtherapy.org/learn-about-therapy/issues/self-compassion.

[97] "What is self-compassion? - Johns Hopkins University Student Well-Being." 04 Dec. 2020, https://wellbeing.jhu.edu/what-is-self-compassion/.

persists with the correct tools. Some of these approaches may be useful if you ever evaluate or criticize yourself for no apparent reason. Some may not be your cup of tea, while others may strike a chord and be useful when you least expect it. According to noted researcher and therapist Dr. Kristin Neff, self-compassion is responding toward oneself as you would a friend when you are having a tough time, failing, or noticing something you don't like about yourself. She even refers to it as "healing ourselves with love." In another corpus of study, Dr. Chris Germer defines self-compassion as a "warmhearted attitude of awareness when we suffer, fail, or feel inadequate." Unlike compassion, self-compassion focuses on our internal relationship with ourselves and our desire to alleviate our pain and suffering rather than putting our own needs on hold.

Self-compassion appears to be a no-brainer. Kindness, tenderness, and empathy for oneself? Please sign us up! So, why is it so difficult to change the story and practice compassion for ourselves? While being compassionate toward others is usually a great thing, being compassionate toward oneself may have a negative connotation by appearing egotistical, self-pitying, or selfish. On the surface, it's simple to agree with that negative logic, but it's just not true. Self-compassion focuses on oneself, but it's done objectively and with mindfulness. It entails facilitating positive momentum rather than engrossing in our ideas and feelings. Recognizing and honoring your most desirable qualities is a healthy and joyful habit. Compassion for oneself is not for the faint of heart. It forces us to think in new ways and might resurrect our past traumatic memories, sentiments, and emotions. Confronting this aspect of ourselves, on the other hand, can be a constructive strategy for long-term recovery.

Tips And Techniques for Practicing Self-Compassion

One smart place to start is to consider how you would treat people you care about. So, while we can't always take away other people's grief, we can validate it and give support to help them grow through it. Allow yourself to make mistakes in this regard. Self-kindness and shared humanity are two distinct but connected concepts: "We're only human. But a) everyone else is, and b) fine." Instead of interpreting our ideas, feelings, and behaviors as who we are, we may absolve ourselves when doing the same for others. For example, if a buddy becomes sluggish and does not return your phone call, you are unlikely to conclude they are a nasty person. Allowing yourself to be human now and then is one approach to embracing your imperfections and reminding yourself that you are not alone in being flawed.

Take care of yourself as you would others. This is closely tied to the last point in that it is about understanding and empathy for oneself. You might physically touch a buddy on the back or hold their hand if they feel depressed, wounded, or unhappy. These, according to Neff, are methods of tapping into our natural "caregiving system" to generate oxytocin, which has good cardiovascular consequences. These acts, along with gentle, forgiving language (even using terms of love to oneself like "darling" or "sweetheart"), can enable us to experience self-kindness even if we are first hesitant. Of course, if it feels too strange, don't go crazy with the affectionate phrases!

Becoming More Self-Aware

Other strategies involve being more self-aware and engaging in self-talk. In contrast to 'beating ourselves up for beating ourselves up,' becoming aware of our internal narratives is a constructive first step toward improving our self-talk.

Make use of 'Releasing Statements.' Perhaps you've never been a big believer in positive affirmations. Perhaps they don't feel natural to you, or you believe they don't 'reach' your Inner Critic on a subconscious level. If that's the case, you may attempt what's known as releasing statements informally.' These are similar to self-forgiveness mini-exercises and draw on the mindfulness notion of detached non-judgment. When you notice yourself thinking anything negative, such as "I'm such a bad person for getting upset," try flipping it around and releasing yourself from the sensation. Instead, say, "It's alright that I was upset."[98][99]

Try accepting yourself. This entails accepting your apparent flaws and character assets (Morgado et al., 2014). Self-compassion is not about exaggerating our flaws to define who we are; rather, thoughts and feelings are behaviors and moods.

Exercise mindfulness. According to Harvard Healthbeat, mindfulness activities might help us focus on the present moment. Not only is mindfulness one of the key components of self-compassion, but many techniques, such as yoga and deep breathing, may be performed at any time and in any place. Kirstin Neff also suggests guided nurturing meditations such as body scans and a brief 'Self-Compassion Break.' Another piece of advice from DiPirro is to quit expecting you'll act in a specific manner. It's easy to make assumptions like "I become incredibly irritable and antisocial on

---

[98] "Self-Compassion: Definition, Examples, and Exercises."
https://www.berkeleywellbeing.com/self-compassion.html.
[99] "Self-Compassion - The Center for Compassion and Altruism Research and ...."
http://ccare.stanford.edu/research/wiki/compassion-definitions/self-compassion/.

flights," which sometimes rules out the chance that you'll behave differently. Instead, it's all about treating oneself as you would others, and it's just a forward-thinking method to benefit yourself from the doubt.

Regaining Perspective

We may also zoom out from here to remind ourselves that we are linked to others. We are part of a much larger picture—common humanity—and we must shift our attention accordingly. Here are a few examples:

Allow yourself to be free of the desire for external validation. Stay Positive, The Positively Present Guide to Life author Dani DiPirro says that most of our negative thinking stems from how others view us. Suppose we're punishing ourselves for eating something, for example. In that case, much of that self-directed rage is motivated by societal expectations, such as the urge to appear a specific way or maintain a certain weight. Therefore, choosing not to bind our happiness to outside forces can be a self-kindness act with far-reaching consequences. If this concept appeals to you, you may learn more in this self-reliance article.

Making an effort to help others. This may be the inverse of the preceding strategy, but it is about setting your sentiments in context. We learn that we are not alone in experiencing pain at different times when we chat with others. It's a vital component in reaffirming our sense of connectivity, reframing our apparent issues in the 'larger picture,' and developing social support networks that are invaluable to our well-being.

We attribute a favorable meaning to individuals who exemplify compassion, and we prefer to think of compassionate people as kind, kind, warm, and empathic. When do you think about such attributes? Who springs to mind? Perhaps it's a prominent person, such as Princess Diana or Mother Teresa, or folks who have been witnessed helping others in need. Maybe your best friend or mother is always there for you when you need it the most. We all know and adore these kind individuals, and they are frequently among the happiest people we know. They brighten up a space and make everyone around them happy. Their caring characteristics come through, but they also produce domino effects and motivate others to do the same. Maybe you consider yourself a sympathetic person, recognizing when someone is in distress and wanting to help them. Many of us, especially empaths, are eager to show warmth and compassion to our close circle of friends, family, and loved ones, moving quickly when we notice their challenges. Instead, we treat ourselves with scorn, anguish, and condemnation. We seek perfection, critique our acts, and set unreasonable goals. Consider communicating to others in the same way you speak to yourself! "Everyone makes errors," we remark when a buddy commits a mistake. When we make a mistake, though, we look at ourselves and exclaim, "You're so foolish!" When a buddy expresses dissatisfaction with their appearance, we respond, "You're so lovely!" However, when we look in the mirror, we frequently feel shame and disgust. Consider how it might feel to speak to yourself in the same manner you communicate to others. Many scholars and psychologists are interested in studying self-compassion, which runs parallel to mindfulness. It pushes us to be nicer, softer in our probably most important relationship: the one we have with ourselves every day.

Like the benefits of being compassionate toward others, practicing self-compassion has several mental and physical health benefits, which is why it is gaining popularity. It has been claimed that practicing self-compassion can help reduce anxiety, despair, and rumination. Furthermore, it helps us connect more profoundly with ourselves and relate to others in new ways as we have a greater connection with their experiences. Developing compassion for oneself in tough or painful circumstances provides several long-term advantages, such as greater motivation, self-worth, overall pleasure, general contentment, optimism for the future, and enhanced resilience.[100][101]

According to Dr. Neff, you should be aware of three aspects of self-compassion as you commence on your path. First, when we feel like we've failed or made a mistake, it's easy to be unkind, harsh, and judgmental of ourselves. Self-compassion teaches us that life is flawed, and that's acceptable. When we accept that terrible times will come to all of us, we may approach ourselves in a kind and gentle manner rather than criticizing ourselves.

Being human entails suffering. While the agony we all go through is unique, it is unavoidable. When we acknowledge that this is a shared experience, we feel less alone and more capable of practicing compassion toward ourselves and others. The COVID-19 pandemic is a prime illustration since the entire world participated in the agony.

---

[100] "4 ways to boost your self-compassion - Harvard Health." 12 Feb. 2021, https://www.health.harvard.edu/mental-health/4-ways-to-boost-your-self-compassion.
[101] "How to Practice Self-Compassion (Article) | Therapist Aid." https://www.therapistaid.com/therapy-article/how-to-practice-self-compassion.

Self-compassion necessitates the capacity to strike a balance between concealing and exaggerating our feelings. In this stage, we must notice our negative feelings and place them in context to avoid becoming engulfed by them.

Developing Self-Compassion

Even if you consider yourself kind, developing self-compassion can be tough, especially at first. It's critical to be patient with ourselves and realize that everything, including ourselves, is a work in progress. Nevertheless, we can all cultivate self-compassion, which will help us live more full, meaningful lives with practice and commitment. Understanding that your practice will not make negative feelings disappear is the first step in cultivating self-compassion. Your practice will assist you in accepting your feelings and pain so that you may move through them more easily. Suppression, on the other hand, will exacerbate them. Self-compassion is closely linked to mindfulness because it helps us gaze within, perceive our inner world, and comprehend where our ideas and feelings are coming from. This permits us to strike a balance between warmth and kindness. It also allows us to be present at the moment and accept a circumstance without judgment. Your realizations will be significant and valuable to your general mindset as you practice mindfulness. Everyone's mindfulness practice will be different, but brief, guided meditations, journaling, or breathing exercises are terrific places to start. You will gradually become more aware of your ideas, feelings, and wants and how they affect your life, both favorably and adversely.

Self-compassion may be tough and unpleasant, but the advantages will help you and the world around you. When we put ourselves first, we put ourselves first in all aspects of our lives. The warmth we feel from compassion for others, and ourselves communicates to the world that we are devoted to long-term health and pleasure.

"Love yourself!" we hear all the time. We are often told that loving ourselves is the most essential and useful thing we can do. But what we don't often hear, or comprehend, is how. What exactly is self-love? What does it mean to put it into practice? How do we get started? Self-love means having a compassionate, kind, patient, tolerable, and curious relationship with yourself. It does not imply that you are so good to yourself that you never accept accountability or responsibility for your faults - "Oh, well, I love myself and think I'm fantastic so that it couldn't be my fault!" Giving oneself compassion and forgiveness when you make errors is part of self-love. It does not imply that you are arrogant or, worse, a narcissist: "I am superior to everyone else, and everyone should try to meet my wants." It is all about believing in yourself and trusting your objectives.[102][103]

Because you can't provide healthy love to others unless you first love yourself, you may feel affection for others, yet you may be afraid to show it. You may love people and wish to relate to them, but you will find it difficult to receive healthy love if you do not first love yourself. In a good relationship, the exchange of love necessitates concrete self-love. Because an empty cup cannot be poured from, consider how much work it takes to show love and affection, be

---

[102] "9 Powerful Self-Compassion Exercises & Worksheets (+ PDF)." 13 Jan. 2020, https://positivepsychology.com/self-compassion-exercises-worksheets/.
[103] "Self-Compassion Quiz | Greater Good." https://greatergood.berkeley.edu/quizzes/take_quiz/self_compassion.

emotionally open, or be attentive. If you don't have reservoirs of self-love within you, your ability to offer love will suffer.

Because self-love heals old scars and traumas, many of us have had challenges that have affected our mental health, sense of self, attitude, and worldview. Traumas can leave us feeling as if we are less valuable than we were before the occurrence. Cultivating our feeling of self-love to originate from inside rather than from elsewhere assists us in moving past previous bad experiences. Because having self-love allows you to establish better, healthier, more true objectives for yourself. How often have you established a goal for yourself based on negativity: disliking your physique, feeling helpless at work, or feeling like a "failure" at a pastime or passion? We want to nurture ourselves rather than "fix" ourselves with arbitrary expectations when we love ourselves. As a result, we have a more accurate understanding of our values and abilities and may decide what is most advantageous to strive towards.

Self-love entails having the same regard and attention for yourself that you have for (and expect from) others. The concept that we should treat ourselves at least and the others in our lives should be easy and uncomplicated, but it isn't always. We occasionally get hung up or trapped on the concept of how self-love or our feeling of worth should seem. We want to love ourselves, yet we find it difficult.

What Gets in The Way of Self-Love?

The voice in your brain that assesses criticizes, and mocks your every move is your inner critic. You are your own greatest adversary when your inner critic is loud and forceful. It hits you where it hurts: the parenting error you made or the meeting you led at work, and it won't let go. Whenever you make an error or say something cruel or inconsiderate because your mood is low, your inner critic gets louder and louder. You're stressed out, and the inner critic gets even louder, and so on. Then, finally, things start falling into place. When you can't stop your inner critic, you carry it with you from place to place, event to event.

There is a fine line between having high expectations and having wildly exaggerated ones. "I will not accept being spoken to disrespectfully" or "I expect the people in my life to respect my boundaries" are examples of self-love standards. Putting oneself under pressure to fulfill unattainable standards is the inverse. When you have unreasonable expectations, you will never be able to meet or maintain them. You then feel inadequate or like a failure. When we have unrealistic expectations, we set ourselves up to "fail" and begin to blame ourselves for not matching up. It is difficult to be gracious to ourselves when we feel inadequate. It is difficult to be patient with oneself when we believe we should have already accomplished a goal. It is difficult to allow ourselves to rest and relax when we do not believe we have succeeded at work or activity. When we devalue ourselves because of perceived flaws, we find it difficult to treat ourselves with respect and care.

Like everything else in life, self-love is a talent that can be learned. Our early life experiences greatly influence how we experience and practice self-love. "Be cautious with how you speak to your child; it becomes their inner voice," I once read online.

It would be much simpler for you to internalize love and self-love if you were talked to with love and compassion as a youngster. It might be challenging to navigate loving oneself as an adult if you did not grow up in a loving atmosphere or if a self-destructive parent raised you. The beauty of self-love is that you already have a lot of kindness inside you because you show it to others. If you are battling with self-love, there is nothing wrong with you. We must be trained as adults to love and care for ourselves. Then, like with any ability, we must practice.[104][105]

The wonderful thing about practicing self-love is that recognizing why we struggle with self-love and where those issues may have started is already an act of self-love. We are doing the work that helps us feel compassion for ourselves by reflecting on our experiences and behaviors. Compassion is a necessary element for honest love.

When we recognize that we require greater self-love, we can begin to conquer the hurdles that stand in our way using skills that can be employed at any time and location. When we apply these skills, we not only treat ourselves with love and care on the inside, but we also start to show that self-love to the outside world. Our ideas become actions, and our acts become our behavior. Our actions determine our standards, and we (and others) are obligated to fulfill them.

Tools to Practice and Strengthen Your Self-Love

Consider what you tell yourself when annoyed, unhappy, or ashamed. Consider speaking those words to a close friend, lover, or family member. Would you do it? Imagine that your friend, lover, or family member is sitting across from you, speaking awful things about him/her/themself. How would you react? In his book "The

---

[104] "Self-Compassion - Emotional Affair." https://www.emotionalaffair.org/wp-content/uploads/2012/10/Self-compassion.pdf.
[105] "Developing Self-Compassion for Beginners - The Wellness Society | Self ...." https://thewellnesssociety.org/self-compassion/.

Feeling Good Handbook," Dr. David Burns includes a technique called "the double standard." He proposes acting as if someone you care about has the same negative self-talk you are. If someone were saying those things to you, write out how you would answer. This is a fantastic technique because it works on many levels. First, it stops thoughts in their tracks when you envision angry or harsh comments about a loved one. Would I approach a buddy in this manner? No. Would I feel comfortable hearing a friend talk about themself in this manner? No. As previously noted, negative self-talk can spiral out of control. Nipping it in the bud might assist in keeping it in check. You have effectively interrupted the narrative, whether or not you have a lot of time to address the topic and assess what you may say to a buddy in a similar position. This is when the tool's next step kicks in, unpacking what was said and reacting with kindness. Even if you don't have time to debrief the experience at the time completely, you may return to it later when you are in a safe location.

You may believe that you would be unable to supply yourself with self-care until you have mastered self-care, but this is not the case. Self-care activities Actions that lead to habits constantly influence your mentality. You may believe that self-care entails "spa days" or being selfish, but this is not the case. Self-care is any activity conducted to address your physical or emotional needs. Self-care is not selfish since it allows you to be the greatest version of yourself. An empty cup cannot be poured from. You must learn to refill your cup; nothing and no one else will be well if you are not well.

While a trip to the spa may be the ultimate act of self-care for some, there are many more ways to care for oneself. You can talk to a friend or loved one on the phone or conduct a little meditation. You may go on a stroll or watch a video on YouTube about unexpected animal friendships. You may create your sleep routine. You can learn how to prepare your favorite cuisine. You may make a list of self-care activities you love and work on crossing them off! Watch a film. Make a list of the things in your life for which you are thankful. Make a bubble bath, light a few candles, and listen to your favorite podcast. The options are limitless, and they are all correct as long as they work for you.[106][107]

Being able to self-advocate is one of the finest methods to improve our self-esteem. We show ourselves care and respect by standing firm and voicing our requirements. Setting limits for ourselves and others is an excellent method to communicate and work toward our goals.

Boundaries are established by first identifying them and then asserting them. The identifying process validates our value in having problems first; through understanding our worth, we cultivate the support and compassion we deserve to provide to ourselves. We define our beliefs and clarify our aims when we set limits; we know what is essential and know ourselves well enough to be realistic about our purpose.

When we declare our limits to others, we find ourselves surrounded by individuals who respect us, generating an environment of respect that we have the emotional support to preserve. A boundary is a form of protection; we protect ourselves by establishing and enforcing a barrier. Consider the persons in your life for whom you feel most

---

[106] "Mindful Self-Compassion | Centers for Integrative Health." https://cih.ucsd.edu/mindfulness/mindful-self-compassion.
[107] "The Five Myths of Self-Compassion - Greater Good." 30 Sept. 2015, https://greatergood.berkeley.edu/article/item/the_five_myths_of_self_compassion.

protective. You understand that you fight to protect them because you care about them. Protecting ourselves in healthy ways via carefully chosen boundaries is a form of self-love.

When we are working on using our self-love engagement tools, it is vital to remember that some days may be more difficult than others to show our self-love. When this happens, we might remind ourselves that "love" and "like" are not synonymous: you probably always love your best friend, even if you don't always agree with their conduct or are irritated that they aren't spending as much time with you right now. But, as with your friendship, you know there is always love there. Remind yourself of the same thing: even when you struggle to use the skills at your disposal or feel like it has faded, love lives inside you. Be kind to yourself; be nice and patient with yourself.

We could not have predicted spending so much time with ourselves a year ago. We have been less "busy" socially, whether alone in lockdown, sharing space with only one other person, or working within a considerably smaller bubble. As a result, we have experienced substantially fewer emotional distractions; for the most part, external validation and stimulation have decreased significantly. This period has most likely resulted in some reflection and self-analysis.

Self-love does not imply that you are completely pleased to be alone; rather, it helps you find inner peace via your ideas. If the last year has taught us anything, it is that the only constant companion we retain throughout our lives is ourselves. Our thoughts and feelings about ourselves will not always be joyous, but our work to be kind and compassionate to ourselves is immeasurable.

Self-love, also known as self-compassion, is attending to your own needs, recognizing your flaws and failings and strengths, and remaining in touch with your emotions. Many people assume that self-love is egoistical because selflessness is such a respected virtue in many communities. Caring for others is crucial, but it should never come at the price of your health. Why? Here are some compelling reasons:

1. Self-care is an important aspect of self-love. When you love yourself, you can spot indications of burnout and take actions to lessen stress. You may not feel you deserve a break if you do not appreciate yourself. It may be difficult to embrace doing something "just for me." As a result, you are more inclined to persevere in the face of adversity. People with strong self-esteem are more inclined to take care of themselves when stressed.

2. According to research, liking oneself might help you make better health decisions. Researchers discovered that when people accepted themselves without harsh criticism, they were more driven to make positive changes in their lives in a Health Psychology meta-analysis of 15 studies. According to one study, this was the case when participants began to quit smoking. Other behaviors included eating more healthfully and exercising. Self-compassion assisted them in developing new, healthier behaviors.

3. It's easy to become depressed during difficult circumstances. Depending on your surroundings, you may encounter people who blame you for your difficulties. You might be blaming yourself. Self-love helps to put things in perspective and counteracts negative, critical self-talk. Even if your

difficulties are the consequence of a mistake you committed, self-love enables you to learn from it and move on. This increases your emotional resilience and prepares you for future difficulties.

4. A popular adage is that you can't fully love people until you love yourself. While this is an exaggeration, liking oneself may help you enhance your relationships with others. When you love yourself, you will be less reliant on others for your feeling of value. This allows you to set boundaries or, if required, end toxic relationships. People who love themselves have a greater understanding of themselves, which helps them determine the types of relationships they desire or do not want.

5. Procrastination kills productivity. You could use harsh measures to motivate yourself. Some people employ threats of self-punishment to get started on a job, but research shows that this is not an effective motivator. When you procrastinate, it's preferable to be kind to yourself. Make your "failure" a learning experience for the future. Instead of being burdened by self-criticism, you'll feel lighter and more prepared to make behavioral adjustments.

6. According to research, those with a high self-compassion are less likely to acquire anxiety or depression. Of course, this does not exclude you from liking yourself if you are nervous or sad. However, it does indicate that parts of self-love (such as self-care, self-compassion, and positive self-talk) might aid in symptom management. Self-love can also help you overcome the frequent misconception that mental illness is your responsibility.

7. Accepting and liking oneself is associated with greater life satisfaction and, as a result, happiness. It's difficult to be happy when you always evaluate your weaknesses and critique your decisions. Self-esteem encourages you to think of yourself as a close friend. You may admit that you are not perfect, yet you still deserve acceptance and support.

8. It's impossible to feel confident when you're constantly criticizing yourself. People who engage in negative self-talk frequently suffer from poor self-esteem. A loss of confidence is the obvious result. Self-love is an excellent approach to training that muscle if you want to feel more confident. Recognize your value and abilities, be gentle when you're upset with yourself and find your confidence growing.

9. Self-love tells you that your dreams are important. Going for what you want in life is not selfish. People may attempt to convince you differently, but as long as you aren't stomping on others to achieve your objectives, you should live your life in a way that makes you happy. Self-love also gives you the resources to achieve your goals, such as less stress, improved emotional resilience, enhanced productivity, and confidence.

10. Self-love may be a difficult idea to grasp. You may be battling the mindset that self-love implies selfishness. The advantages of self-love that we've discussed thus far may not be persuasive enough. Consider this: loving yourself benefits others. Self-love, like enjoyment, can be contagious. It helps people understand why having a healthy connection with yourself is vital if you demonstrate it. They'll start practicing

self-care and self-compassion. When you love yourself, you benefit everyone around you, not just yourself.[108][109][110]

For many reasons, self-love is essential for happiness in your life. Self-love is described as a conscious decision to care for and compassionately treat oneself first and foremost. On a deeper level, self-love is caring more about your well-being. Self-love manifests itself as trusting yourself, expressing boundaries, and an overall greater connection to oneself, which may lead to connections with others. Self-love may also entail being compassionate to oneself and prioritizing rest when necessary.

It might be difficult to realize how vital loving oneself is.... but what can happen when you don't provide self-love is much more difficult. Your happiness is determined by how you care for yourself, and self-love has been related to enhanced resilience and the ability to perceive things from a different angle. When you put yourself last or fail to appreciate yourself, you will experience greater tension, worry, and overreaction to minor issues you may have previously dismissed. As a result, things will get increasingly difficult and stressful, leaving you exhausted and unhappy.

You're working more hours from home...and feeling the strain. Being in severe need of vacation yet unable to justify taking time off for oneself. You lower your voice and agree to request time off when "everyone" on the team is available. At the same time, you feel

---

[108] "How to practice self compassion and tame your inner critic." 18 Jun. 2021, https://www.betterup.com/blog/self-compassion.
[109] "The power of self-compassion - Harvard Health." 02 Feb. 2022, https://www.health.harvard.edu/healthbeat/the-power-of-self-compassion.
[110] "Self-compassion - Wikipedia." https://en.wikipedia.org/wiki/Self-compassion.

obligated to be there for your children, husband, and closest friend, who is going through a difficult period. You're under pressure to help everyone, but you're not getting enough sleep and aren't taking care of yourself since it appears as if everyone needs you. Feeling resentment and wondering why you're upset or perhaps angry. You feel as if you've lost your voice and no one cares.

You feel you lack empathy for others, but you don't say anything because you don't want others to think you're selfish.... and you realize you worry a lot about what people think and say about you. The fact is that self-love is tough to acquire, and it requires effort and practice to keep loving yourself consistently. Many individuals feel bad about putting themselves first. On the other hand, self-love is important to your pleasure and progress. True, discovering techniques to supply self-love is exceedingly difficult; nonetheless, there are several reasons why self-love is vital to your pleasure. When we understand why self-love is vital for ourselves, we can enjoy our pleasure regardless of what is happening in our world. Continue reading to discover why it is vital to embrace self-love for enhanced pleasure in your life. Some Important Reasons Self-Love is Required for Happiness:

To Liberate Yourself from Comparisons

Who and why do you compare yourself to? When we compare ourselves to others, we set ourselves up for failure. Why? People who genuinely love themselves understand that comparing never feels good... but they still do it. "Comparison is the thief of pleasure," Teddy Roosevelt famously remarked... and he's completely correct!! How often have you scrolled through social media and watched a friend talk about their "ideal" life? The lovely house, the automobile, the perfect happy family... You don't know that that family may be conducting their family therapy on the inside, and they are about to lose their house, causing tension and fights. They recently signed up for marriage counseling, are considering divorce, and haven't had sex. The lesson is that what appears on the surface may not represent what is going on behind the scenes... and it's fine... But here we are, comparing our lives to their "beautiful image," feeling jealous and worse than we did an hour before scrolling.

To Live Life in Alignment with Values

What are your core beliefs? Are they related? Friends? Success? Kindness? If you are not practicing self-love, it is quite likely that one or more of these areas are deteriorating. For example, your "family" values may not align with your current life because you lack self-love. You may find that you are having difficulty being present with your family and are missing out on precious moments or that you just do not have the energy for them. Or maybe your value is kindness, but you've become more frustrated or quick to respond... and you can't be nice right now... Why? Because you're running on fumes, and everyone else is receiving your affection but you. In anxiety and depression treatment, I examine values to determine what is important to you in your life and how to assist you in identifying gaps where you are not living by those values. A lack of self-love frequently causes a lack in these areas. Understanding what you value may be eye-opening and inspiring to start reclaiming your happiness and living the life you desire.

Confidence

Consider someone who is self-assured... How do they behave? Do they appear to be certain of their beliefs? Do they make use of their voice? Are they also good listeners? Self-love boosts self-confidence since it allows you to accept yourself... just as you are. You're not so focused on your weaknesses or that you stumbled over certain sentences during your zoom training. Being human and self-forgiving. When you allow yourself to embrace all of who you are, you will discover that you no longer feel ashamed or insecure about not being someone else. I encounter many clients who have lost confidence due to a lack of self-love in my practice. Many of them are unaware of it. Also, if they are harsh or critical of themselves, they are likely to be harsh on others. When you can begin to show compassion to yourself, especially through difficult moments, you will build confidence and, as a result, boost your pleasure. Allow us to assist you on your trip. [111][112]

Resilience Through Challenges

Let's face it, and the globe is in a bad way! We are confronted with unprecedented problems... It's common to struggle with COVID19, social distance learning, and attempting to balance working from home and running a household. However, when we experience adversity, we often grow. We recognize our power and learn to view adversities as lessons or "lily pads" to help us advance in life. For example, when you understand self-love, you will be able to forgive yourself more quickly and realize that things will work

---

[111] "What is Self-Compassion? Components, Myths, and Strategies." 27 Jun. 2012, https://psychcentral.com/blog/5-strategies-for-self-compassion.

[112] "Self-Compassion | Trauma Recovery." https://trauma-recovery.ca/recovery/self-compassion/.

out. In addition, you will learn to speak to yourself as you would to a loved one or a tiny child...with love, kindness, and a calm tone.

Maintain Healthy Relationships

Self-love improves connections, whether with friends, family, or romantic relationships. People are taught how to treat us by ourselves. If we don't respect and love ourselves, others may feel free to do the same to us. When you love yourself, you set the standard for how you'll tolerate being treated in any relationship. Our sense of self-worth is tested when we are subjected to abuse. How well-defined are your boundaries? Do you enjoy making other people happy? To prevent saying "yes" to something when you meant "no," or allowing someone to mistreat you, you must learn to trust yourself and use your voice to express what is best for you. When you genuinely love yourself, you have no patience for others who do not appreciate or cherish you. You will also learn to create limits and safeguard your energy.

CHAPTER 7

Self-Awareness

There are many different aspects of oneself that one must be aware of to be self-conscious. Anxiety is a mental state in which a person feels as if they are the focus of attention. Self-awareness appears early in the development of the self-concept. You may value self-awareness, but it's not the only thing on your mind. On the other hand, self-awareness becomes woven into who you are and emerges at different moments depending on the scenario and your personality. People are not born fully self-aware. However, research has shown that newborns have a fundamental understanding of their existence. Infants are aware that they are distinct from others, as indicated by actions such as the rooting reaction, in which a newborn reaches for a nipple when anything brushes against their face. In addition, researchers discovered that even babies could distinguish between self and non-self contact.

Self-awareness is the ability to monitor your feelings and reactions. It enables you to identify your strengths, weaknesses, triggers, motivators, and other traits. Being self-aware entails looking at your emotions, why you feel the way you do, and how your feelings might manifest as reactions. Self-awareness helps you react better to events or individuals that may irritate you, which is a valuable talent, especially as a leader. When you are conscious of your emotions and how you deal with them, you will be better able to process and work through them, preventing unneeded confrontation. This can also help you set a positive example for your staff, making them feel more comfortable approaching you with queries or concerns. Even if you aren't where you want to be as a leader, establishing self-awareness and recognizing opportunities for improvement is the first step.[113][114]

Leaders who lack self-awareness may look arrogant. How can you lead a firm if you can't be personable or recognize when you've crossed a line? Other work scenarios necessitate self-awareness as well. Consider how important self-awareness is while presenting sales pitches or dealing with feedback; if you are unaware of how you will respond or do not have a strategy to prevent a bad reaction, you might get yourself into trouble. Presentations benefit from self-awareness as well. Many people become uncomfortable before giving proposals, speeches, or simply meeting notes. Self-awareness can be beneficial. If you find too many filler words during

---

[113] "Self-Compassion - an overview | ScienceDirect Topics."
https://www.sciencedirect.com/topics/psychology/self-compassion.
[114] "What is Self-Confidence? - University of South Florida."
https://www.usf.edu/student-affairs/counseling-center/top-concerns/what-is-self-confidence.aspx.

presentations, rehearse your speech and have someone clap every time you use a term you want to avoid. If you sway or pace around when speaking, you can restrict your capacity to move by sitting at a table with your client or utilizing a podium.

What are Self-Awareness Skills?

Self-awareness is understanding how you will react to others in addition to being aware of your feelings. "Self-awareness keeps us anchored, tuned in, and focused," Campbell writes in her book. "Grounded leaders are more efficient and deliberate in remaining on target and aware of others." In addition, leaders who can regulate their brains and emotions enable people around them to achieve their self-awareness and success." These are some crucial self-awareness abilities:

1. **Empathy:** You will become more empathic as you improve your self-awareness because of increased emotional intelligence.

2. **Adaptability:** If you know how you would respond, you may avoid a difficult scenario by going for a stroll or just taking a few deep breaths.

3. **Confidence:** Accepting and even loving your shortcomings, needs, and talents increases your ability to be vulnerable, allowing for deeper working interactions. Maintaining confidence is essential for success.

4. **Mindfulness:** When you are self-conscious, you become more aware of the current moment, allowing yourself to respond to things as they occur rather than lingering on the past or projecting into the future.

5. **Patience:** While your initial impulse may be to criticize an employee for a mistake or vent on your team, self-awareness will allow you to exercise patience even amid disagreement.

6. **Kindnes**s is possible when you put your sentiments aside to help someone else. Even if you're having a horrible day, being self-aware and understanding that your coworkers are also human beings experiencing similar difficulties might help you be more compassionate.

Tips for Becoming More Self-Aware

Being self-aware isn't always simple, but it may help you become a more successful leader. Here are some suggestions for increasing self-awareness.

Maintain an open mind. When you successfully govern your emotional environment, you may be more sensitive to the feelings of others. In addition, to be a good leader, you must be interested in new individuals and what they offer. This demonstrates that you can work well with others and not always have to be the star.

Be aware of your talents and shortcomings. Self-conscious individuals know their skills and flaws and can operate from that position. Being aware of this means knowing when to seek help and when you can manage a problem on your own.

Maintain your concentration. Making relationships is a vital element of being a leader, but you can't do it if you're distracted. Improve your productivity by training yourself to focus for long periods without being distracted by social media, emails, or other little distractions.[115][116]

Establish limits. A leader must establish firm boundaries. Be kind to others but firm when necessary. Maintain the integrity of your objectives and the work you put into them by being serious about your job and hobbies.

Understand your emotional triggers. Self-aware individuals may recognize their feelings as they occur. Instead of suppressing or denying your feelings, bend and flex with them and thoroughly understand them before speaking with others.

Accept your intuition. Successful people learn to trust their intuition when making decisions and accept the risks of such decisions. Your instincts are driven by the urge to succeed and the survival of the fittest. They will advise you on what to do next, so learn to trust your instincts.

Exercise self-control. Good leaders are disciplined in all aspects of their lives. This quality gives them the long-term concentration required for effective leadership.

We frequently behave without first thinking, focused solely on our wants. While admitting your emotions is necessary for self-awareness, you must also analyze how you deal with those feelings and how your following actions affect people around you. Being more respectful of others will assist you in navigating challenging situations.

---

[115] "What Is Self-Confidence? | HealthyPlace." 04 Jun. 2022, https://www.healthyplace.com/self-help/self-confidence/what-is-self-confidence.
[116] "What is Self-Confidence? + 9 Ways to Increase It [2019 Update]." 22 Dec. 2020, https://positivepsychology.com/self-confidence/.

When necessary, apologize. Mistakes happen, but being self-aware can help you identify when you need to apologize. For example, maybe you yelled at your coworkers or have been difficult to contact recently. Whatever your error was, the best approach to go ahead is to apologize (and mean it) and then change your behavior.

Request feedback. While the notion of self-awareness is to comprehend yourself without the help of others, asking for honest employee feedback requires bravery (and self-awareness). This acknowledges your inherent prejudices toward oneself (which we all have) and assists you in gaining a more objective perspective.

Another phrase that gets bandied about a lot in the psychology profession is "self-awareness." So, what is it exactly? Stepping back and witnessing your thoughts and feelings as they emerge is a sort of self-awareness. It might be as easy as observing your feelings when you spend time with specific individuals or the ideas that pass through your mind when you are afraid to attempt something new. It may also be a more comprehensive, layered understanding of how your ideas influence your emotions, physical experiences, and behaviors. For example, you may realize that you are uninspired about the day ahead. Your body may feel heavy, and your energy may be low, causing you to stay in bed longer than you expected, triggering thoughts about how trapped you are and how difficult the day ahead will be. Self-awareness is the ability to shine a light on aspects of your mental world that may otherwise be buried, pushed aside, or go unnoticed. Your "internal world" is psychological jargon for your ideas, feelings, bodily experiences, and drives. The first step toward transformation and progress is being aware of these characteristics of yourself. After all, you can't fix what you don't understand.[117][118]

Self-Awareness Takes Courage

It takes courage and can be challenging and uncomfortable at times. You could even wonder why you thought this was a good idea in the first place! But, as the name implies, self-awareness turns your focus away from what's going on around you and onto yourself. So, rather than focusing on what other people do and say – such as "my partner doesn't get it," "my parents put too much pressure on me," or "my employment is uninteresting" - the emphasis is on how you think and feel. It is a change in emphasis from what is going on around you to what is going on within you.

When you take a step back and contemplate, you will learn new things about yourself. Some things will appeal to you, while others will not. Our worries, inadequacies, regrets, failures, and defects coexist with our talents, accomplishments, and lighter side. When you practice self-awareness, you're more likely to tap into the most difficult, humiliating, confused, and overpowering aspects of yourself. If you're not thinking to yourself, "wow, I wish I hadn't done that," or "I don't like the way I spoke to that person, then" you're probably concealing from certain aspects of yourself. As you become more acquainted with these "darker" aspects of yourself, your inner critic will likely emerge, and a powerful sensation of guilt

---

[117] "How to Build Self-Confidence - Stress Management from Mind Tools."
https://www.mindtools.com/selfconf.html.
[118] "How to Boost Your Self-Confidence - Verywell Mind." 14 Feb. 2022,
https://www.verywellmind.com/how-to-boost-your-self-confidence-4163098.

may ensue. The inner critic thrives on guilt and may be a powerful force that stifles our desire to be self-aware.

Taking Care of Yourself is Crucial

As you shine a light on aspects of your internal reality that seem uncomfortable and challenging, you must balance this with self-care and self-compassion. Self-awareness without self-compassion is a sure formula for feeling bad about oneself. Remember that self-awareness is not the same as self-judgment. Self-awareness requires honesty, but it requires a large dose of self-compassion and self-care. It is critical to consider how you will ground and calm yourself if you feel overwhelmed or agitated by what you become aware of throughout this process. It's always a good idea to enhance your abilities in dealing with severe emotions before going on the road of self-awareness.[119][120]

Contradictions are Normal and Human

One of the most exciting aspects of growing in self-awareness is seeing how much conflict resides inside you. Your worldview shifts from black and white to grayscale. You become aware of the grey that surrounds you. For example, instead of solely communicating with your parents for the reasons you love them, you may be more open about the aspects you struggle with and dislike. Alternatively, you may feel thrilled and energized about an approaching work

---

[119] "How To Build Self-Confidence in 7 Steps | Indeed.com." 13 Aug. 2021, https://www.indeed.com/career-advice/career-development/how-to-build-self-confidence.
[120] "What is Self Confidence and Why is it Important?." 25 Apr. 2019, https://cognitiveheights.com/what-is-self-confidence-and-why-is-it-important/.

presentation yet fearful and unmotivated. When you find yourself experiencing such contradicting ideas and sensations, you may feel guilty and puzzled at first, but with time, this understanding appears to feel liberating.

Most of us will have a part of us that resists the concept of being more honest with ourselves about what we think and feel. This is reasonable. Simply put, these are our defense systems at work. This is our mind's attempt to keep us from confronting aspects of ourselves that we don't like, don't want to admit, or find too painful or frightening. Take your time learning about yourself in this way. Self-awareness is a lifelong exercise that should not be rushed or bulldozed, especially if you have a history of trauma. Rushing through may cause you to fall or throw in the towel entirely. Instead, small, sustainable steps are essential, and professional advice and direction are sometimes required.

The Role of Self-Awareness in Therapy

The advantages of treatment range from person to person. Regardless of the benefits and changes that clients experience, enhanced self-awareness appears to be a basic component of why the treatment works for most individuals, at least anecdotally. This makes sense since self-awareness is the starting point for better understanding ourselves and our relationships, improving our mental health and wellness, and having a life that feels full and expansive.

Being a psychologist is an extremely fulfilling profession. However, when a client begins to truly feel into their self-awareness and apply this information to improve their life, it is one of the most rewarding moments in therapy. Self-awareness is one of those abilities that appears to prepare you for all of life's obstacles. It is a gift to observe someone embracing all aspects of who they are and seeing its impact on their lives.

How Do You Become More Self-Aware?

This is a large question with a far larger solution. The possibilities for increasing our self-awareness are limitless. This isn't a "how-to" post; rather, it's an exploration of the concept of self-awareness. Some of the ways we can improve our self-awareness are through journaling, meditation, mindfulness, the breath, speaking with people we trust, seeing a therapist, trying new things, the arts, paying attention to our dreams, taking risks, allowing ourselves to fail, speaking up, and sitting in stillness. An easy technique to start practicing self-awareness is to check in with yourself regularly and ask yourself:

- What feelings are present?
- What am I experiencing in my body at the moment?
- What do I want to accomplish or do as a result of how I think and feel?
- What are the thoughts that are going through my head? What am I telling myself?

Of course, self-awareness is not the only factor contributing to transformation and progress. Many other things are required to change some of the issues and recurring patterns in our lives, but self-awareness appears to be the critical first step on this vital route.

The term "mindfulness" refers to focusing on the here and now rather than allowing one's thoughts, meditations, or daydreams to take over one's thoughts and actions. When you meditate, you let your thoughts come and go without holding on to anything in particular, such as a mantra or your breath. Both techniques can assist you in being more aware of your internal state and reactions to situations. They can also assist you in identifying your thoughts and feelings and avoiding being so engrossed in them that you lose sight of your "self."

Yoga is a physical exercise, but it is also a mental one. Your mind develops discipline, self-acceptance, and awareness while your body is stretching, bending, and flexing. As a result, you become more aware of your body and all the sensations that arise and your mind and thoughts. Yoga can even be used with mindfulness or meditation to increase self-awareness.[121][122]

Reflecting may be done in various ways (including writing; see the next point), but the key is to look through your thoughts, feelings, and behaviors to evaluate where you met your standards, fell short, and could improve. You might also examine your standards to determine if they are appropriate for you to hold yourself to. You can reflect on yourself by writing in a diary, talking aloud, or simply sitting quietly and pondering.

Writing in a journal has the benefit of helping you become more aware of, clear up, and accept your thoughts and feelings. When

---

[121] "12 Tips For Building Self-Confidence and Self-Belief (+PDF Worksheets)." 16 Jan. 2022, https://positivepsychology.com/self-confidence-self-belief/.
[122] "Why Self-Confidence Is More Important Than You Think." 20 Sept. 2018, https://www.psychologytoday.com/us/blog/shyness-is-nice/201809/why-self-confidence-is-more-important-you-think.

you use this tool, it's easier to discover your ideal life goals and the things that are important to you personally. Helps determine what is not important, insignificant, and does not work for you. Both are essential to understand. Writing down your ideas and feelings, whether in free-flowing posts, bulleted lists, or poems, helps you become more conscious and deliberate.

It is critical to believe we know ourselves from the inside, but external feedback is also beneficial. Inquire about your relatives and close friends about what they think of you. Allow them to describe you and discover what rings true and what shocks you. Consider what they say and keep it in mind when you journal or otherwise ponder. Of course, don't take anyone's word for it; you need to speak with various individuals to obtain a whole picture of yourself. Remember, at the end of the day, your self-beliefs and sentiments are most important to you!

Importance in Counseling and Coaching

Self-awareness is a valuable technique that, when used frequently, may benefit coaches and clients more than anything else a professional can teach them. People must be able to gaze within and get familiar with their internal world to effect true, permanent change.

Building self-awareness should be the first goal for almost all clients, followed by more typical coaching and counseling sessions. You may, for example, coach someone on their negative behaviors and provides 1,000 strategies to break them. Still, if they don't understand why they have these poor habits in the first place, it's practically a certainty that they will either never change them or will quit for a while and just start up where they left off when circumstances become rough.

Self-awareness is essential not just for the coachee or client but also for the coach or counselor. Self-awareness is a top priority for the counseling profession, according to the Council for Accreditation of Counseling and Related Educational Programs Standards (2017), since it is both a requirement for counselors and a critical skill to impart to their clients.[123][124]

It needs a high level of self-awareness to deliver competent guidance and actionable advice. Furthermore, self-awareness will prevent the caring counselor from becoming overly involved in their client's troubles or viewing the issues through their distorted lens. To properly assist someone, it is necessary to see things from their perspective, which necessitates being self-aware enough to set our ideas and feelings aside at times.

Self-Awareness Emergence

According to studies, a more complicated sense of self-awareness begins to form about one year of life and becomes more developed by 18 months. Lewis and Brooks-Gunn researched the development of self-awareness. The researchers used a red dot to mark an infant's nose before holding the youngster up to a mirror. Children who identified themselves in the mirror reached for their noses rather than their reflections, indicating that they had some amount of self-awareness. However, Lewis and Brooks-Gunn discovered that

---

[123] "Self-confidence Definition & Meaning - Merriam-Webster."
https://www.merriam-webster.com/dictionary/self-confidence.
[124] "65 Synonyms & Antonyms of SELF-CONFIDENCE - Merriam-Webster."
https://www.merriam-webster.com/thesaurus/self-confidence.

nearly no youngsters under one year would reach for their nose instead of their image in the mirror.

It is crucial to note that the Lewis and Brooks-Gunn research only shows an infant's visual self-awareness; infants may have other types of self-awareness even at this young age. Researchers Lewis, Sullivan, Stanger, and Weiss, for example, proposed that expressing emotions requires self-awareness and the ability to think about oneself about other people.

Self-Awareness Development

Researchers believe that the anterior cingulate cortex, which is located in the frontal lobe region of the brain, plays a key role in the development of self-awareness. Brain imaging studies have also revealed that this area gets engaged in self-aware individuals. According to the Lewis and Brooks-Gunn experiment, self-awareness appears in children at 18 months, which coincides with the fast expansion of spindle cells in the anterior cingulate cortex. However, one research discovered that a patient preserved self-awareness despite significant brain injury to the insula and anterior cingulate cortex areas. This shows that certain brain regions are not necessary for most elements of self-consciousness and that awareness may instead result through interactions scattered across brain networks.

Self-Consciousness

People might become extremely self-aware at times, resulting in self-consciousness. Have you ever felt that everyone was watching you, assessing your actions, and anticipating your next move? This increased self-awareness might make you feel uneasy and nervous in particular situations. In many circumstances, these emotions of self-consciousness are only fleeting and occur while we are "in the limelight." On the other hand, excessive self-consciousness might be a symptom of a persistent disease such as social anxiety disorder. These individuals are more aware of their sentiments and views and hence are more inclined to adhere to their ideals. They are, however, more prone to have negative health repercussions such as increased stress and worry.

People who are self-conscious in public have a greater level of public self-awareness. They are more concerned with how others see them and are frequently anxious that others are evaluating them based on their appearance or conduct. As a result, these people tend to adhere to social standards and avoid circumstances where they can appear terrible or feel ashamed.[125][126][127]

Self-awareness is essential for understanding ourselves and relating to others and the world. Being self-aware allows you to compare yourself to others. Excessive self-consciousness can occur in those with an extraordinarily strong sense of self-awareness. If you believe you are battling a self-consciousness that negatively impacts your life, talk to your doctor about your symptoms to learn more about how to manage these feelings.

---

[125] "self confidence Crossword Clue | Wordplays.com."
https://www.wordplays.com/crossword-solver/self-confidence.
[126] "Self-Confidence in the Workplace: Why It's Important and How To Improve ...." 10 Mar. 2021, https://www.indeed.com/career-advice/career-development/self-confidence.
[127] "How to Build Self Confidence (with Pictures) - wikiHow." 16 Apr. 2022, https://www.wikihow.com/Build-Self-Confidence.

CHAPTER 8

Self-Exploration

It takes a lifetime to discover your genuine self. It does not happen in a single day or epiphany, yet it is still worthwhile to pursue. When you discover your actual self through self-discovery, you know what you're supposed to accomplish and are no longer fearful. You can conquer anything if you rise with sincerity. What is your authentic self? Is it the person you used to be? When were you the happiest? When did you learn that crucial life lesson? When did you reach that goal? When did you assist that stranger? Or when you performed by your ideals regardless of what others expect? The truth is that all of these elements combine to form your genuine self. The key is not to find your actual self. It's reminiscing.

Many of us live our lives only scratching the surface of our identities. We do not delve deeply enough into our ideas, feelings, desires, and dreams. One of the issues is that we are constantly on the move. When the to-do list grows longer, self-exploration takes a back place. How could it not, when we hardly have time for ourselves? Self-exploration entails "looking at your ideas, feelings, actions, and motives and asking why." According to Ryan Howes, Ph.D., a psychologist, writer, and lecturer in Pasadena, California, "it's digging for the roots of who we are answers to all the questions we have about." There are several advantages to having a better awareness of oneself. It "assists people in understanding and accepting who they are and why they do what they do," he says, "which enhances self-esteem, communication, and relationships." Howes outlines how he helps clients investigate their own identities, the various barriers to self-exploration, and ways readers may attempt at home.[128][129]

"What have you discovered about yourself this week?" That's the question Howes usually asks at the beginning of a session. As he put it, this investigation exemplifies the enormous quantity of material just waiting to be investigated, which is "revealing itself all the time." He also focuses on emotions, which he describes as "the most direct and primitive representation of the self." As a result of his work, "clients can understand their feelings better, how they manifest physically in their bodies, and the context they first experienced those feelings." However, the task does not end there. Outside of treatment, Howes recommends that clients "write, exercise,

---

[128] "14 Methods to Dramatically Increase Your Self-Confidence." https://www.cornerstone.edu/blog-post/14-methods-to-dramatically-increase-your-self-confidence/.
[129] "How to Build Self-Confidence - Verywell Health." 15 Nov. 2021, https://www.verywellhealth.com/how-to-build-self-confidence-5209231.

meditate, or pray, and explore creative pursuits such as artwork, writing, dancing [or] music."

Howes is frequently confronted with three impediments to self-discovery. First, as previously said, our hectic lifestyles might cause us to lose touch with ourselves. "Our exterior world is so busy, so full of stimuli, that prying ourselves away long enough to take a good look within is a great problem," he remarked. What is the solution? He advised people to unplug, take a break, and simply be. For example, Howes assigns some clients to sit for 10 minutes and simply be with themselves, without "doing anything, falling asleep, watching TV, or whistling a song."

Second, self-discovery is tiring. "It's difficult to revisit traumatic memories, face the realities of our limits, or accept the risk of making a difficult decision." However, in this situation, practice is beneficial. "Self-exploration is similar to working out in that it becomes easier with consistency." Every day, Howes advised readers to check in with themselves (at the same time, if you prefer). "What am I observing about myself today?" you might ask yourself. Finally, for some people, prior trauma might stymie self-discovery. "Sometimes the mind closes the door to painful memories, and no matter how hard we try, we can't get in."

Nevertheless, you can heal, even if it is difficult. Finding an experienced trauma therapist is an excellent place to start. Here are some self-exploration techniques to get you started:

Act Authentically

You become your genuine self when you act truthfully. Instead of being concerned, you are traveling with knowledge. Because they know you're trustworthy, people come to you. You have flaws, yet you persevere. You are enough as you are and as you are. When you are authentic, your decisions are shaped by who you are. Nothing can bring you down if you're true to yourself and don't let go of who you are. You're not looking for external validation, and understanding what you have enables you to do more with what you have. Those around you benefit from your genuine concern for their well-being since you care more about what's best for themselves than theirs. A better self-result in a better world.

Use Self-Affirmations

"I am sufficient," you say. I am powerful. I am not a victim; I am a victor. I've got what it takes. I shall triumph. I shall persevere even when it appears impossible. I am not flawless, but I am human. Therefore, I am permitted to relax rather than resign. I'm not the only one. I'm ok. I am thankful. "I'm at ease." You accept these statements as true when you utter them. You become them after feeling them. Finding your genuine self via self-exploration leads to discovering your true self. Obstacles and opposition will move out of the way once you tell the world who you are. When you are self-assured, you see possibilities, lessons, and knowledge.

Confront Your Inner Critic

Nothing would ever get done if everyone only listened to the negative voice in their thoughts. If Einstein had listened to his instructor, who once told him that he didn't have what he needed, he would not have developed the Theory of Relativity and much more. The world would be deprived of individuals who could have made such a difference. Fear of the unknown, not being good enough, or loss and lack fuels the inner critic. On the other hand, fear does not have to dictate what happens. By not listening to your inner critic, you may overcome fear. Instead, acknowledge your inner critic and add, "I imagine what COULD happen..." to turn a negative situation into a good one. Fear may remind you to wear your seatbelt, rehearse before performing, make wise decisions, and so on, but it does not have to rule you. It may not disappear when you meet your inner critic, but you may comfort it and eventually release it.[130][131]

Don't Hide Your Imperfections

It's simple to put on a mask and declare, "This is who I want others to think I am." Instead, it's more satisfying to remove the mask and declare, "This is who I truly am, and I am proud of that person." You may live freely by owning who you are if you engage in self-exploration. This will make you more accountable and influential. People will listen when you tell your story and speak your truth, and they will be motivated to uncover their truth. Then, self-discovery can spread.

Find Who You Are Not

Find out who you are, NOT if you want to know who you are. What aspects of your history have shaped your present? What about your

---

[130] "Building Confidence and Self-Esteem | Psychology Today." 30 May. 2012, https://www.psychologytoday.com/us/blog/hide-and-seek/201205/building-confidence-and-self-esteem.

[131] "Self Confidence | Definition, Importance for Career, Ways to Improve." https://www.cleverism.com/skills-and-tools/self-confidence/.

culture, religion, family, friends, neighbors, and so on? What exactly are you, and what exactly are they? You'll never be finished learning yourself, but you may utilize differentiation to become independent by distinguishing yourself from what isn't you by tracing the roots of your beliefs. When you distinguish, you do not disregard or reduce the impact of previous events. What are your distinct objectives, interests, values, and ideas? Begin by determining what you are not. Self-exploration is a voyage of discovering how and by what you have been molded and molded throughout your life. It's fine that things inspired you, but have you ever wondered why? How can you know what you are and what you aren't if you can answer that question?

Log Your Life

Journaling is an excellent tool for self-discovery. To get started, all you have to do is start putting your thoughts down. If you're at a loss for ideas, consider writing about the following: Make a mental note of the time and place. What is it that makes you feel better or worse? What are your stressors? What makes you successful? When you figure out what makes you tick, you can better manage yourself and your life. You have a secure zone where you can be yourself, and you only post entries if you are comfortable doing so. You may pour it out daily or just check in. You may also notice what's happening around you, allowing your thoughts to wander and flow. Allow for pauses and moments of introspection before returning to your work. Allow the conclusion to emerge organically when you feel you have nothing left to say. If you maintain a record, you may understand how your mind works and identify harmful habits, which can help you reclaim control of your life. More advantages of journaling may be found here.

Focus On What is Right with You

Perhaps your mind ruminates what you dislike about yourself and what you believe others dislike. Perhaps you believe that chances pass you by because you are unworthy. Everyone has a negativity bias, which causes them to believe more in the negative than the good at first. Recognizing that your mind may be deceiving you is the first step toward recognizing the truth. When you focus on what is best for you, you combat the beliefs that enforce the belief that you have nothing to contribute. You have more influence over your situation if you control what you think. Have you ever complimented yourself? You may personalize it by saying, "I enjoy how you care for other people." You have a fantastic attitude. When horrible things happen, you always rise. "I adore you."

Find Solace in Solitude

Unplugging and getting away might be beneficial for self-exploration. You will feel better if you go outside into nature and invest in yourself. Make time to meditate and focus solely on yourself rather than the world around you. Pay attention to your thoughts rather than what others are saying. When you check-in, you re-discover yourself. Recharging may not alter everything or put an end to the challenging situation, but it can help you acquire the mentality and energy to confront it with inner strength.

Practice Self-Care

When individuals try to relax, they frequently experience guilt and anxiety. You may be on vacation, but your mind is not. Allowing yourself to relax will allow you to fight your fights more effectively and plunge deeper into self-exploration. Self-care will see more breakthroughs than self-sabotage. It's not only about pampering yourself when you practice self-care. It takes time to do what is necessary to be who you need to be. Each person defines self-care differently. It might be utilizing essential oils and taking a bath for some. Others may see it as a hike into nature, away from your issues and troubles. Know that you deserve self-care in whatever form it takes for you.

Try Mindfulness

Being present and at the moment is an excellent technique to train your mind to avoid catastrophizing. When you fail, you don't declare to yourself, "I'm a failure." Mindfulness assists you in stopping self-judgment by simply monitoring your thoughts and interrupting negative thinking patterns. Consider your ideas to be like leaves blowing in the air. Place each idea on a leaf and let it pass. You do not need to be linked to each one. Instead, practice deep breathing, which stimulates the Vagus nerve and relieves tension and stress. As you exhale, note how the leaves move away from you until they are in the distance. When your supervisor is talking over you and wants to raise your voice, you may be aware. You can be attentive to your children when they beg for their sibling's toy, and you just want to give in to put an end to it. You may stay attentive even in the most stressful moments, giving you a chance to review the situation. Whatever the scenario, you calm down to act with a clearer head and make the best decisions.[132][133]

---

[132] "Building Your Self-Confidence - Mind Tools."
https://www.mindtools.com/downloads/lbr5283hs/BuildingYourSelfConfidence.pdf

[133] "Self-Confidence: Definition, Affirmations, and Tips for Gaining ...."
https://www.berkeleywellbeing.com/self-confidence.html.

Self-discovery looks different for everyone, but honesty always leads you back to yourself. When figuring out who you are, you must start with what is important to you. You must examine your values, which will provide you with the criterion for life. Most importantly, self-discovery is about self-love.

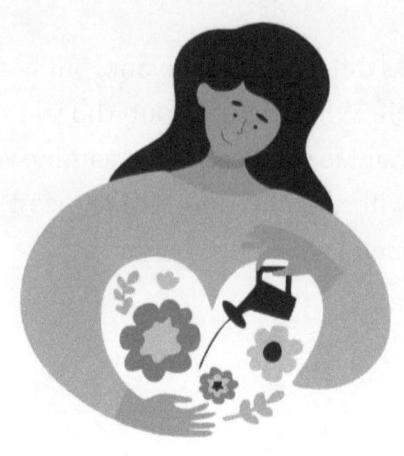

CHAPTER 9

Self-Care

While many individuals consider self-care a selfish luxury, it is an integral aspect of a person's overall well-being. Self-care has become a popular buzzword in recent years, but many people are still unsure. Continue reading to learn more about self-care and why it is so important for your mental and physical health. Self-care is defined as "the ability of people, families, and communities to promote health, maintain health, prevent disease, and cope with illness and disability with or without the assistance of a healthcare practitioner." Therefore, the primary purpose of self-care is to prevent or control sickness and maintain general well-being by the continual act of taking care of one's health in numerous dimensions.

What Are the Barriers to Self-Care?

While self-care may appear simple and uncomplicated, several hurdles might restrict or prohibit someone from practicing it regularly. Some examples of self-care obstacles include:

Low self-worth: According to a study, persons who are highly critical of themselves or have a low sense of self-worth generally avoid or do not prioritize self-care.

Feeling guilty: Putting others first is normal for many people, especially those who have children or are used to caring for others due to their life or job position. However, when they are entrusted with taking care of themselves, they feel guilty because they believe they are being selfish.

Time constraints: Life becomes hectic, and self-care is frequently pushed to the bottom of the priority list while seemingly more vital tasks go incomplete.

Making change isn't easy: You will need to make certain lifestyle modifications to implement self-care techniques. Unfortunately, this is not a simple task.

A lack of understanding: Many individuals mistake self-care for frivolous expenditure; however, this is not the case. People are less likely to conduct regular self-care if they do not understand the greatest and most helpful types of self-care.

Workplace culture surrounding self-care: There is a stigma associated with self-care in some organizations, as though practicing it is inherently selfish. While this is not the case, it frequently leads to people viewing self-care as a stressor due to how their colleagues perceive it.[134][135]

A lack of planning: Most people conduct self-care only when it is essential, resulting in ineffective self-care activities. While there is no one impediment to self-care, many people suffer from a loss of self-worth, which leads to a lack of self-care. This is because individuals do not believe they deserve to prioritize themselves and their health, or they do not believe they are deserving of self-care routines.

What Types of Self-Care Are There?

There are several types of self-care that include diverse activities or acts. Each kind is equally vital and contributes to overall health and well-being. Self-care includes taking care of one's physical wellbeing. This might include getting enough exercise, eating a diet rich in nutrients and whole foods, or engaging in soothing hobbies that can assist with stress management. Getting enough sleep is also part of physical self-care. Mental self-care promotes mental health by engaging in brain-stimulating activities and healthy mental habits. Having good relationships is a type of self-care in and of itself. According to research, many types of relationships, whether romantic, platonic, or family, may all boost general health and well-being. Research shows that they are more likely to be in good physical and mental health than their single counterparts when it

---

[134] "What is Mindfulness? - Mindful." 08 Jul. 2020, https://www.mindful.org/what-is-mindfulness/.
[135] "Mindfulness journal."
https://binaries.templates.cdn.office.net/support/templates/en-us/tf34169450_wac.docx.

comes to married couples. Married couples are also less likely to become ill or die from disorders such as cancer, heart attacks, or surgery. While successful marriages are related to good overall health, unhealthy relationships and marriages are not. According to research, the quality of a romantic relationship is closely tied to a person's health.

Solid social ties are also associated with greater overall health, and studies have shown that having a good network of friends may considerably enhance a person's physical and mental health. Conversely, people who lack spiritual ties are more prone to experience psychological discomfort and participate in risky behaviors.

Finally, maintaining healthy familial ties is self-care since it promotes excellent health. For example, coping with a chronic illness and having a strong family support system has improved disease outcomes.

What Are the Benefits of Self-Care?

Self-care daily can result in both short- and long-term advantages that contribute to better well-being and health condition. For example, people who practice self-care may see the following benefits:

- Putting your health and needs first and getting some rest may drastically lower stress levels.
- The better you feel about yourself, the better you will feel about yourself. This is because more of your essential demands will be satisfied regularly.

- In the case of good relationships, spending time with loved ones will offer you sentiments of belonging and affection, which is beneficial to your general mental health.
- Improved disease and chronic illness management
- Disease prevention in the future
- It can help minimize chronic stress, which can contribute to chronic illness.
- Better relationships as a result of increased self-esteem and self-worth
- an increase in work satisfaction
- Reduced burnout as a result of life's activity
- Overall increased life quality and well-being

Self-care has several advantages, including enhanced work and social connections, reduced chronic illness risk or symptoms, and a higher quality of life.

How to Build a Self-Care Plan

Creating your ideal self-care strategy will be dependent on your health and lifestyle. To develop a strategy to promote greater health and well-being, you will:

1. **Determine your overall level of health:** Once you've determined your starting place in terms of health, you may start adding or removing particular activities or stresses from your life.

2. **Identify your stressors:** Create a list of all the things in your life that make you anxious. After that, you can do your

hardest to avoid specific pressures. However, if they are inevitable, you may train yourself with coping methods to help you cope with stressful situations.

3. **Identify your coping strategies:** Everyone develops coping mechanisms to deal with health challenges, stress, and other life issues. Make a note of your coping mechanisms and determine which are healthy and not. The ones that aren't serving you because they're unhealthy will need to be replaced with healthier coping techniques.

After that, you can create a strategy from your lists that you can genuinely commit to. If you have a chronic condition, your self-care routine may differ from that of someone who does not. This is just because you will need to combine some beneficial activities. For example, if you have diabetes, you will want to make sure that your self-care coping skills and activities assist you in managing your condition while adhering to your treatment plan. Self-care has become a popular phrase in recent years, but many people are unaware of it. While retail therapy and spending your funds on vacation may appear to be acts of self-care because they make you feel better in the moment, they are not. Self-care is more of a lifestyle shift that allows a person to make time for their health to secure their general well-being now and in the future. If you use the proper self-care strategies, you will be able to reap the advantages, such as improved physical and mental health, illness prevention or management, and improved personal and working connections. Making self-care a priority can be challenging, especially if you are busy and have always placed yourself last. The most crucial aspect of self-care is that it is not selfish. It is a crucial tool that promotes general health and should be at the top of everyone's priority list. After all, if you don't take care of yourself now, it will be far more difficult to do so later.[136][137][138]

All the stress-relieving activities in the world won't assist you if you don't care for yourself. For example, meditation will be useless if you aren't getting enough sleep. If you try to meditate, you may fall asleep since you aren't meeting your body's demand for sleep. Similarly, going to the gym once in a while won't do much good if you don't eat healthily regularly. Therefore, if you want your stress reduction exercises to be effective, you must prioritize your fundamental necessities. This book explores many sorts of self-care and why they are so important. It also discusses some of the steps you may take to create your self-care strategy.

The definition of self-care is "a multidimensional, multilayered process of deliberate participation in techniques that promote healthy functioning and increase well-being." Essentially, the phrase refers to a deliberate action taken by a person to enhance their physical, mental, and emotional wellness. Self-care may take many different forms. It might be as simple as getting enough sleep each night or walking outdoors for a few minutes to catch some fresh air. Self-care is essential for developing resilience in life's unavoidable pressures. You'll be more equipped to live your best life if you've made efforts to care for your mind and body.

---

[136] "Mindfulness | Psychology Today."
https://www.psychologytoday.com/us/basics/mindfulness.
[137] "Mindfulness Definition | What Is Mindfulness - Greater Good."
https://greatergood.berkeley.edu/topic/mindfulness/definition.
[138] "Mindfulness exercises - Mayo Clinic." 15 Sept. 2020,
https://www.mayoclinic.org/healthy-lifestyle/consumer-health/in-depth/mindfulness-exercises/art-20046356.

Unfortunately, many individuals regard self-care as a luxury rather than a necessity. As a result, they are overloaded, tired, and ill-equipped to deal with life's inevitable obstacles. To ensure that you're taking care of your mind, body, and spirit, it's important to assess your self-care practices in various areas.

Self-care is more than just finding ways to unwind. It is about caring for oneself on all levels: cognitively, physically, emotionally, socially, and spiritually. To care for your health and well-being, you must strike a balance that allows you to handle each of these areas. Sometimes extra self-care in one area is required to restore balance or find respite from a stressor in your life.

Maintaining a healthy physique is essential if you want it to work correctly. Keep in mind that your body and mind are inextricably intertwined. Taking good care of yourself will improve your mood and outlook on life. Physical self-care entails nourishing your body, how much sleep you receive, how much physical exercise you do, and how well you look after your physical requirements. Attending medical visits, taking prescribed medications, and monitoring your health are all examples of effective physical self-care.

Self-care requires socialization. However, it is frequently difficult to make time for friends, and it is tempting to forget your connections when life becomes hectic. Close relationships are essential for your well-being. The most successful technique for creating and maintaining intimate connections is to devote time and effort to forming relationships with other people. You don't have to spend a certain amount of time with your friends or work on your relationships to improve them. Everyone's social demands are slightly varied. The goal is to identify your social requirements and make time in your schedule to have an ideal social life.

Your mental health is strongly influenced by the thoughts and ideas that occupy your mind. Quizzes and learning about a topic that interests you are examples of mental self-care activities. Reading or watching uplifting movies or novels can re-energize you. Mental self-care includes whatever you do to help keep your mind healthy. Self-compassion and acceptance, for example, can assist you in maintaining a better inner dialogue. According to research, a religious or spiritual lifestyle is often healthier.[139][140]

On the other hand, nurturing your spirit does not entail religion. It can include everything that aids in the development of a greater feeling of meaning, comprehension, or connection with the cosmos. Spiritual self-care is essential, whether you love meditating, attending religious services, or praying.

It is critical to have good coping skills while dealing with unpleasant emotions such as anger, worry, and grief. An example of an emotional self-care activity is anything that helps you acknowledge and express your feelings regularly in a secure environment. For emotional self-care, whether you talk to a loved one or engage in leisure activities that help you process your feelings, it's essential to incorporate these activities into your daily routines and schedules.

A good self-care regimen should be personalized to your lifestyle and requirements. It must be something you produced for yourself. Creating your self-care strategy might serve as a preventative tool to keep you from being overwhelmed, overstressed, or burned out. Determine which aspects of your life require greater attention and self-care. And evaluate your life regularly. As your circumstances

---

[139] "Mindfulness - Wikipedia." https://en.wikipedia.org/wiki/Mindfulness.
[140] "What Is Mindfulness? | Taking Charge of Your Health & Wellbeing." https://www.takingcharge.csh.umn.edu/what-mindfulness.

change, so will your self-care requirements. The following stages can help you develop your self-care plan:

- **Assess your needs:** Make a list of the many aspects of your life and the primary activities you perform each day. Work, school, relationships, and family are a few examples.
- **Consider your stressors:** Consider the features of these areas that produce stress and how you may manage that tension.
- **Devise self-care strategies:** Consider some activities that will help you feel better in each area of your life. Spending time with friends or establishing limits, for example, can help you form good social bonds.
- **Plan for challenges:** Create a strategy for change when you realize you're ignoring a certain element of your life.
- **Take small steps:** You do not have to take on everything simultaneously. Instead, determine one simple move you can do to begin properly caring for yourself.
- **Schedule time to focus on your needs:** Make self-care a priority even if you don't think you have time for anything else. When you care for all elements of yourself, you will discover that you can function more successfully and efficiently.

The responsibilities of your everyday life might influence the sort of self-care you require the most. For example, a self-care strategy for a busy college student who is always cognitively engaged and has a thriving social life may need to prioritize physical self-care. On the other hand, a retired person may need to plan more social self-care to ensure that their social demands are addressed. Self-care is not a one-size-fits-all approach. Self-care is a process that must be adjusted to your own needs and circumstances. You don't want to wait until you've hit rock bottom. The idea is to take measures every day to ensure that you are getting what you need to deal with the stress and hardships of everyday life.[141][142]

Let's clear up one prevalent mistake right away: Self-care does not imply self-indulgence or selfishness. On the contrary, taking care of oneself is essential if you want to be healthy and productive at work, help others, and do the other things you set out to do in a day. You are correct if you believe you have heard more about self-care recently. One indicator: the number of searches for "self-care" has more than doubled since 2015, according to Google Trends. Paula Gill Lopez, Ph.D., is an associate professor and chair of the psychological and educational counseling department at Fairfield University in Connecticut when it comes to self-care. Anxiety and sadness are on the rise, she continues. "Everyone feels it." In the words of Kelsey Patel, author of Burning Bright: Rituals, Reiki, and Self-Care to Heal Burnout, Anxiety, and Stress, self-care is a part of the solution to how we may all better cope with the everyday problems that confront us. A work-related stressor. Technology has quickened the speed of modern life more than ever before, making it even more difficult to maintain pace (just think how many emails come flooding into your inbox each day). "People feel lonelier and less able to unwind and calm down, which makes even the simplest chores feel more tense and overwhelming," Patel adds. At Everyday

---

[141] "How to Practice Mindfulness - Mindful." 12 Dec. 2018, https://www.mindful.org/how-to-practice-mindfulness/.

[142] "How to Practice Mindfulness: 11 Practical Steps and Tips." 06 Oct. 2021, https://positivepsychology.com/how-to-practice-mindfulness/.

Health, self-care is doing your best to meet your physical and emotional health requirements.

When defining self-care, some organizations and scholars use a health-oriented approach. For example, according to this organization, the World Health People, families, and communities can promote health; prevent disease; keep healthy, and manage illness and disability with or without the support of a healthcare practitioner. This concept encompasses everything connected to keeping physically healthy, such as cleanliness, eating, and obtaining medical treatment when necessary. In addition, it refers to all of the measures a person can take to manage stresses in their life and care for their health and well-being.

Some researchers have used a clinical approach in the same way. For example, 2010 research published in the JBI Library of Systematic Reviews defined self-care as "the collection of activities in which one performs throughout life daily," emphasizing promoting health, preventing illness, and dealing with difficulties. In April 2018 research published in BMC Palliative Care, self-care was defined as "the self-initiated action that people include to enhance excellent health and overall well-being." The study's authors stated that it is not just about being healthy but also about implementing coping skills to deal with workplace challenges. For example, self-care includes getting vaccinated, scheduling cancer screenings, and taking prescription prescriptions on time – but healthcare professionals and organizations also have a role in how successfully people engage in these self-care behaviors. In other words, there are several persons and things that influence any one person's ability to engage in self-care.[143][144]

Self-care definitions have grown increasingly applicable to the general population as it has become more mainstream, focusing on tuning in to one's needs and satisfying them. Marni Amsellem, Ph.D., a licensed psychologist in Trumbull, Connecticut, defines self-care as "whatever you do for yourself that feels nutritious." "That might be something pleasant or peaceful, or it can be something intellectual, spiritual, physical, or something you need to get done," she explains. According to the International Self-Care Foundation, health literacy is also a pillar of self-care. Any measures you take toward better-comprehending health information you need to make appropriate decisions about your health and well-being qualify as self-care. As a result, at Everyday Health, self-care is defined as all of the measures you take to care for your physical and mental health in the ways that you are best equipped to do so.

---

[143] "The Benefits of Mindfulness - Verywell Mind." 15 Oct. 2021, https://www.verywellmind.com/the-benefits-of-mindfulness-5205137.
[144] "Benefits of Mindfulness: Mindful Living Can Change Your Life." https://mindfulness.com/mindful-living/benefits.

CHAPTER 10

Self-Esteem

Motivation, mental health, and quality of life may improve if you have a healthy sense of self-worth. However, it is possible to have dangerously high or low self-esteem. You can find the right balance for yourself if you know how much self-esteem you have. In psychology, "self-esteem" refers to a person's overall subjective perception of their value. In other words, self-esteem may be described as how much you like and value yourself regardless of your circumstances. Many variables influence your self-esteem, including:

- Self-confidence
- Identity
- Feeling of security
- Feeling of competence
- Sense of belonging

Self-esteem is frequently used interchangeably with self-worth, self-regard, and self-respect. Self-esteem is lowest in childhood and rises over adolescence and adulthood, finally reaching a reasonably stable and long-lasting level. As a result, self-esteem is similar to the consistency of personality traits across time.

Why Self-Esteem is Important

Self-esteem influences your decision-making, relationships, emotional health, and general well-being. It also impacts motivation since people who have a healthy, positive self-image recognize their potential and may be encouraged to take on new tasks. People who have a positive self-image:

- Have a good grasp of their abilities
- Because they have a good connection with themselves, they can maintain healthy relationships with others. In addition, they have realistic and reasonable expectations of themselves and their skills.
- Understand and can articulate their wants

People who have poor self-esteem are less confident in their talents and may question their decision-making process. They may lack the motivation to try new things since they do not believe they can achieve their objectives. People who have poor self-esteem may struggle with relationships and communicating their needs. They may also have poor self-esteem and feel unlovable and worthless. People with excessive self-esteem may overestimate their talents and believe they are entitled to success even if they lack the necessary qualifications. Because they are preoccupied with perceiving themselves as ideal, they may struggle with interpersonal troubles and avoid self-improvement.[145][146]

Many theorists have written about the dynamics of self-esteem growth. Abraham Maslow's hierarchy of needs places self-esteem at the top of the most important human motivations list. Humans, according to Maslow, must have both external and interior self-esteem to achieve a sense of self-worth. For a person to develop as a person and attain self-actualization, both of these conditions must be satisfied. It is vital to distinguish self-esteem from self-efficacy, which is concerned with how well you feel you will manage future actions, performance, or talents. Healthy self-esteem may assist and encourage you to achieve your objectives since it allows you to navigate life knowing that you can achieve everything you set your mind to. Furthermore, having high self-esteem allows you to set appropriate boundaries in relationships and maintain a healthy relationship with yourself and others.

Low self-esteem has been linked to several mental health conditions, including anxiety and depressive disorders. It may also be tough to achieve your objectives and maintain good relationships. Low self-esteem can negatively influence your quality of life and raise your chances of having suicidal thoughts. Overly high self-esteem is sometimes mislabeled as narcissism, although there are several key differences between the two. Individuals with narcissistic qualities may have high self-esteem, but their self-esteem

---

[145] "Mindfulness & Meditation - Harvard University." https://www.harvard.edu/in-focus/mindfulness-meditation/.
[146] "12 Fun Mindfulness Exercises - The American Institute of Stress." 10 Feb. 2021, https://www.stress.org/12-fun-mindfulness-exercises.

is fragile and fluctuates depending on the environment. Too much self-esteem can lead to interpersonal issues, difficulties in social situations, and an unwillingness to tolerate criticism.

Low self-esteem can cause or exacerbate mental health issues such as anxiety and depression. Consider consulting with a doctor or therapist about available treatment choices, including in-person or online psychotherapy, drugs, or a mix of the two. You may do actions to improve your self-esteem, even though some of the root reasons for poor self-esteem, such as inherited qualities, childhood trauma, and personality traits, are beyond your control. Keep in mind that no one is more deserving than anybody else. Maintaining a positive self-image may be easier if this is kept in mind.

Your feeling of self-worth will influence every aspect of your life. Your career, relationships, and even physical and mental health reflect your self-esteem. But what shapes your perception of yourself and your abilities? Because of the way you've been treated in the past and the decisions you've made in your life, your self-esteem may have increased or fallen. The good news is that you have a decent degree of power over enhancing your sense of self-worth. You may challenge your mind and body by making tiny, real adjustments. Take measures to eliminate negative thinking and increase good, encouraging ideas about the person you are and can be.

Replace Negative with Positive Thinking

1. **Identify triggers:** To enhance your degree of positive thinking in your daily life, you must first understand who, where, and what promotes negative thinking. Maybe it's

your bank account balance or a coworker who is always moaning. Certain things cannot be changed, but how you react to and comprehend them can. Paying attention to what makes you unhappy or worried is the first step.

2. **Take notes:** As you go about your day, your brain is always engaged in a dialogue or "self-talk." This self-talk examines the environment and develops judgments about yourself and others. So, start observing any noteworthy tendencies in this conversation. For example, do facts support this thinking? Or does it tend to be unreasonable, constantly expecting the worst in a situation?

3. **Challenge your thinking:** If you see yourself leaping to conclusions or downplaying the positive aspects of yourself, it's time to step up and include some positive thinking into your self-talk. Learning to focus on the good and encourage oneself is similar to building muscles. You must train your brain daily to build the ability to think positively, forgive yourself when you make errors, and learn to give yourself credit when you achieve a goal.

If you're not sure where you stand regarding self-esteem, making a list of your attributes will assist. If you find yourself listing more flaws than virtues, this might indicate that you are overly harsh on yourself. Instead, consider what qualities, abilities, and hobbies you haven't yet mentioned or found. Never think you know everything there is to know about yourself and your capabilities. Every day, people with high self-esteem allow room for self-discovery.[147][148][149]

People who have poor self-esteem sometimes reject their triumphs as luck or accident. Alternatively, they may focus on their shortcomings rather than their achievements. On the other hand, people that have strong self-esteem enjoy their successes. When others admire them, they respond "Thank you" rather than ignoring the comment. This is not to say that persons with high self-esteem are arrogant or egotistical; they simply believe in their skills and recognize triumphs when they occur.

Other individuals cannot be the benchmark for your self-esteem. This is because there will always be someone who looks better or more capable than you in whatever aspect of life. Social media doesn't help either, as studies discovered that those who check social media regularly are more likely to have poor self-esteem. Remind yourself that most individuals just post the highlights of their lives on social media. Your own life should be the yardstick, not the lives of others, since what is best for you may not be best for someone else, and vice versa. Finally, remind yourself that you are making progress every time you improve or prevent yourself from making the same error.

The more you show that you cherish your health, the more you acquire the ability to love other aspects of yourself. Pay attention to your body's signals and avoid meals that make you irritated or weary.

---

[147] "6 Mindfulness Exercises You Can Try Today." 27 Oct. 2017, https://www.pocketmindfulness.com/6-mindfulness-exercises-you-can-try-today/.

[148] "22 Mindfulness Exercises & Activities for Adults (+ PDF)." 06 Feb. 2022, https://positivepsychology.com/mindfulness-exercises-techniques-activities/.

[149] "Mindfulness.com - #1 App for Mindful Living, Meditation, & Breathwork ...." https://mindfulness.com/.

Eating healthily and exercising might also help you think positively and feel more optimistic about your future. Spending time with individuals who care about you may make it unexpectedly simpler to care for yourself. Remember that establishing positive thinking skills and healthy living practices will not happen overnight. It takes time, effort, and patience to be kind to yourself and increase your feeling of self-worth. However, the more you question your views and viewpoints, the more pride you will have in yourself and your talents. You'll be proud of how far you've gone and excited about the future.

Many of us understand the importance of boosting our self-esteem. In addition to feeling better about ourselves, having a high level of self-esteem also makes us more resilient. According to a brain scan study, we are more likely to heal from emotional scars like rejection and failure if we have a greater sense of self-worth. In addition, when we have better self-esteem, we are less prone to anxiety; when we are stressed, we produce less cortisol in our circulation, and it is less likely to persist in our system. However, as lovely as it is to have more self-esteem, it turns out that increasing it is a difficult undertaking. Despite the seemingly limitless supply of articles, programs, and products promising to boost our self-esteem, the fact is that many of them do not work and may even make us feel worse.

Part of the difficulty is that our self-esteem is inherently fragile, fluctuating daily, if not hourly. To complicate matters, our self-esteem includes our overall sentiments about ourselves and how we feel about ourselves in certain areas of our lives (e.g., as a father, a nurse, an athlete, etc.). The more significant a single domain of self-esteem, the greater its influence on our overall self-esteem. Having someone grimace when they taste the not-so-delicious supper you made will affect a chef's self-esteem far more than it will hurt someone whose identity does not include food.[150][151]

Finally, having high self-esteem is beneficial, but only in moderation. Extremely high self-esteem, such as that of narcissists, is frequently exceedingly frail. Such people may feel good about themselves most of the time. Still, they are also particularly susceptible to criticism and negative feedback and respond in ways that stifle their psychological self-growth. That being said, it is feasible to boost our self-esteem if we approach it correctly. Here are some suggestions for boosting your self-esteem when it is low:

Use Positive Affirmations Correctly

Positive affirmations like "I will be a tremendous success!" are immensely popular. Still, they have one major flaw: they make individuals with poor self-esteem feel even worse about themselves. Why? Because such assertions are simply too counter to our previous views when our self-esteem is low. Positive affirmations, ironically, work for one subset of people – those with strong self-esteem. So, when your self-esteem is low, modify your affirmations to make them more credible. For example, instead of saying, "I'm going to be a huge success!" say, "I'm going to endure until I succeed!"

---

[150] "Reduce Stress Through Mindfulness - Whole Health." https://www.va.gov/WHOLEHEALTH/features/Reduce_Stress_Through_Mindfulness.asp.
[151] "What is mindfulness? - Mind." https://www.mind.org.uk/information-support/drugs-and-treatments/mindfulness/about-mindfulness/.

Identify Your Competencies and Develop Them

Self-esteem is developed through exhibiting genuine skill and accomplishment in areas of our lives that are important to us. For example, if you take pride in your cooking ability, have more dinner parties. Sign up for races and train for them if you're a decent runner. In short, identify your key abilities and seek chances and occupations that would enhance them.

Learn to Accept Compliments

It's tough to boost self-esteem because when we're feeling down about ourselves, we're more averse to receiving compliments. So, set yourself the objective of enduring compliments, even if they make you nervous (and they will). Set responses are the simplest way to avoid instantly ignoring praise (e.g., "Thank you" or "How kind of you to say"). In addition, the desire to downplay or reject praises will lessen with time, which is also a good indicator of growing self-esteem.

Introduce Self-Compassion, Not Self-Criticism

We are more likely to injure our self-esteem when we have a low sense of self-worth. Because our objective is to boost our self-esteem, we must replace self-criticism (which is usually always unproductive, even if it seems persuasive) with self-compassion. Specifically, if your self-critical inner monologue arises, ask yourself what you would say to a close friend in your circumstances (we are far more sympathetic to friends than ourselves), and direct those words to yourself. This will prevent you from further harming your self-esteem with critical thoughts and will instead assist in building it.

Affirm Your Real Worth

The following activity has been shown to help restore your self-esteem after a setback: Make a list of the traits you possess relevant to the scenario. For example, if you were rejected by a date, list attributes that make you a good relationship prospect (such as loyalty or emotional availability); if you were passed over for job advancement, describe qualities that make you a great employee (you have a strong work ethic or are responsible). Then, for one of the things on your list, write a small essay (one to two paragraphs) explaining why the attribute is valuable and likely to be valued by others in the future. Finally, do the exercise every day for a week or anytime you need to increase your self-esteem. The basic line is that raising self-esteem takes some effort since it entails creating and sustaining healthy emotional habits, but doing so, especially successfully, will deliver a significant emotional and psychological return on your investment.

Self-Esteem Check

Self-esteem is the whole total of your thoughts and feelings about yourself, including how you regard your strengths and weaknesses. When you have a strong sense of self-worth, you believe that you are worthy of respect from others and deserve it. When you have poor self-esteem, you respect your opinions and thoughts less. You may be continually concerned that you are not good enough. Here's how to detect whether your self-esteem is low and why it's critical to cultivate a strong sense of self-worth.[152][153]

Relationships with individuals close to you – parents, siblings, friends, instructors, and other significant contacts — are critical to your self-esteem. Many of your current views about yourself result from signals you've gotten from these folks throughout time. If your connections are good and you consistently receive favorable feedback, you are more likely to regard yourself as valuable and have higher self-esteem. Conversely, you are more prone to battle with low self-esteem if you receive predominantly negative feedback and are frequently chastised, taunted, or disrespected by others. However, your prior experiences and relationships do not have to be your fate. Your ideas have the most influence on your self-esteem – and you have power over them. Modifying your tendency to focus on your shortcomings or weaknesses might help you establish a more balanced, truthful perspective of yourself.

Range of Self-Esteem

Depending on your circumstances, your self-esteem will change over time. It's natural to have periods when you feel bad about yourself and feel great about yourself. However, self-esteem often remains in a range that represents how you feel about yourself overall, and it rises somewhat with age. Consider how to identify your self-esteem extremes:

---

[152] "Mindfulness: How It Helps Your Health - WebMD." https://www.webmd.com/balance/guide/what-is-mindfulness.
[153] "Mindfulness for Beginners | Psychology Today." 12 Jul. 2017, https://www.psychologytoday.com/us/blog/how-be-yourself/201707/mindfulness-beginners.

1. **Low self-esteem:** When you have poor self-esteem, you don't value your views and opinions as highly. You emphasize your perceived flaws and shortcomings while downplaying your strengths and abilities. You feel others are more capable or accomplished than you. You may find it challenging to accept favorable remarks. You may be afraid of failure, which might prevent you from achieving at your job or school.

2. **Healthy self-esteem:** Healthy self-esteem indicates that you have a balanced and truthful picture of yourself. For example, you may believe in your strengths but realize your weaknesses.

It's difficult to have too much self-esteem when it's wholesome and anchored in reality. Boasting and feeling superior to others is not an indication of excessive self-esteem. It's more likely an indication of insecurity and poor self-esteem.

Benefits Of Healthy Self-Esteem

You feel comfortable and worthwhile when you regard yourself and have high self-esteem. You have typically favorable interactions with people and are self-assured in your talents. You are also receptive to learning and feedback, which may aid in acquiring and mastering new abilities. With good self-esteem, you're:

- Don't be shy in expressing what you're thinking and feeling.
- You are confident in your decision-making abilities.
- Capable of forming trusting and honest relationships — and less likely to remain in toxic ones

- Expectations should be realistic, and you should be less judgmental of yourself and others.
- More robust and able to withstand stress and setbacks

Self-esteem influences almost every aspect of your life. Maintaining a healthy, realistic image of oneself does not imply extolling your virtues. It's about learning to accept and respect oneself despite your flaws.[154][155]

Low self-esteem may have a detrimental impact on almost every aspect of your life, including your relationships, employment, and health. However, you may improve your self-esteem by taking cues from many mental health therapies. Consider the following steps, which are based on cognitive behavioral therapy. First, pay attention to your ideas regarding troublesome situations after you've identified them. This involves what you tell yourself (self-talk) and how you interpret the circumstance. Positive, negative, or neutral ideas and beliefs are all possible. They might be reasonable, based on logic or facts, or irrational, based on incorrect assumptions. Check to see whether these beliefs are correct. Would you tell a friend these things?

Your initial opinions may not be the only way to perceive a situation, so examine their correctness. Consider if facts and logic support your point of view or whether alternate explanations for the situation are possible. Be mindful that it might be difficult to detect mistakes in reasoning. Even if they are views or perceptions, long-held ideas

---

[154] "Mindfulness - Mental health and wellbeing | healthdirect." https://www.healthdirect.gov.au/mindfulness.
[155] "Meditation - Mayo Clinic." 05 May. 2022, https://www.mayoclinic.org/tests-procedures/meditation/about/pac-20385120.

and thoughts might feel natural and true. Pay attention to mental patterns that undermine self-esteem as well:

- Think everything or nothing. You either perceive everything as all nice or all negative. "I'm a huge failure if I don't do this assignment," for example.

- Mental sifting. You only perceive negatives and focus on them, altering your perception of a person or circumstance. "Because of my error on the report, everyone will know that I'm not up to running this company." for example.

- Positives are being turned into negatives. You dismiss your accomplishments and other pleasant experiences by claiming that they don't matter. "I only performed well on that test because it was so simple," for example.

- Making unfavorable assumptions. When there is little or no evidence to support your conclusion, you form a negative conclusion. "My buddy hasn't responded to my email, so I must have done something to irritate her," for example.

- Mistaking emotions for facts. You mix your emotions or views with facts. "I feel like a failure; thus, I must be a failure," for example.

- Negative self-talk. You undervalue yourself, cast yourself down, or make fun of yourself. "I don't deserve anything better," for example.

Adjust Your Thoughts and Beliefs

Replace any negative or incorrect thinking with accurate, helpful thoughts. Try the following strategies:

- Use optimistic statements. Kindness and encouragement should be extended to oneself. Instead of worrying that your presentation will fail, tell yourself, "Even though it's difficult, I can handle this circumstance."
- You must forgive yourself. Everyone makes errors, and those mistakes do not define you as a person. They are separate periods. "I committed a mistake, but that doesn't make me a horrible person," tell yourself.
- Should and must expressions should be avoided.
- Concentrate on the good. Consider the aspects in your life that operate nicely. Consider the abilities you've developed to deal with difficult situations.
- Rename troubling ideas. It is not necessary to respond badly to unfavorable ideas. Instead, consider negative thoughts to be cued to attempt new, healthier routines. "What can I do to lessen the tension in this situation?" ask yourself.
- Motivate yourself. Give yourself credit for making progress. "My presentation might not have been great, but my colleagues' asked questions and remained interested – which suggests I met my aim," for example.

You might also attempt these acceptance and commitment therapy-based steps.[156][157]

Consider the settings or situations that appear to decrease your self-esteem. Pay attention to your ideas regarding troublesome situations

---

[156] "How to Meditate - Mindful." https://www.mindful.org/how-to-meditate/.
[157] "Meditation | Psychology Today." https://www.psychologytoday.com/us/basics/meditation.

after you've identified them. Repeat your negative ideas aloud or write them out unexpectedly, such as with your non-dominant hand. Consider seeing your negative ideas inscribed on various items. You could even imagine yourself singing a song about them. These activities might help you observe and take a step back from habitual thoughts and beliefs. Instead of modifying your ideas, try to separate yourself from them. Recognize that they are nothing more than words. Accept bad ideas or sensations rather than battling, rejecting, or being overwhelmed by them. You don't have to like them; only allow yourself to be moved by them.

Negative ideas do not have to be managed, altered, or acted upon. Instead, reduce the potency of your negative thoughts and their impact on your conduct. You may counteract or adjust your thinking about the ideas and beliefs contributing to your low self-esteem as you become more aware of them. This will assist you in accepting your worth as a person. As your self-esteem grows, so will your confidence and sense of well-being. In addition to these tips, strive to remember daily that you are deserving of particular attention. To that end, remember to: Look after yourself. Follow solid health advice. Try to exercise for at least 30 minutes every day of the week. Consume plenty of fruits and veggies. Limit your intake of sweets, junk food, and animal fats. Do things you like. Begin by developing a list of your favorite activities. Then, every day, try to do something from that list. Spend time with individuals who bring you joy. Don't waste time on folks who are rude to you.

Confidence in one's worth as a human being is a valuable psychological resource and a generally positive aspect of life; it is associated with accomplishment, healthy relationships, and fulfillment. Conversely, with low self-esteem, people may feel sad, fall short of their potential, or accept abusive relationships and conditions. It can also be a hallmark of clinical narcissism, in which people are self-centered, arrogant, and manipulative. Perhaps no other self-help issue has given rise to much advice and many (sometimes contradictory) theories. Your self-esteem is your assessment of yourself. People with healthy self-esteem are proud of themselves and their accomplishments. While everyone has moments of insecurity, those with low self-esteem are uncomfortable or dissatisfied with themselves most of the time. This can be improved, but it requires time and effort regularly. If you are having difficulty boosting your self-esteem or if low self-esteem is producing difficulties such as depression, consult your doctor for information, guidance, and referral.[158][159][160]

---

[158] "Meditation - Wikipedia." https://en.wikipedia.org/wiki/Meditation.
[159] "Meditation: In Depth | NCCIH." https://www.nccih.nih.gov/health/meditation-in-depth.
[160] "Meditation: Take a stress-reduction break wherever you are - Mayo Clinic." 29 Apr. 2022, https://www.mayoclinic.org/tests-procedures/meditation/in-depth/meditation/art-20045858.

Conclusion

There are a lot of discussions these days about self-love. It sounds nice, but what exactly does it mean? How do we love ourselves, and why is it important? Self-love entails accepting yourself, treating yourself with compassion and respect, and nurturing your growth and well-being. Self-love includes how you treat yourself and think and feel about yourself. So, when you think about self-love, consider what you would do for yourself, how you would communicate to yourself, and how you would feel about yourself that expresses love and concern.

When you love yourself, you have a good outlook on yourself. This does not imply that you are always pleased with yourself. That would be impossible! For example, I may be sad, furious, or dissatisfied with myself while loving myself. If this is unclear, consider how this works in other partnerships. For example, I can love my son even when I am upset or unhappy with him. Even in the middle of my rage and disappointment, my love for him shapes how I interact with him. It enables me to forgive him, respect his feelings, address his needs, and make decisions that benefit his health. Self-love is extremely similar. You may improve your connection with yourself if you learn to love yourself and practice self-love. This is essential if you want to form good relationships with others. Self-love does not develop quickly, but you will grow better at it with time. Even if you're stressed, consider how far you've come. When you eventually learn to be kind to yourself, you will be one step closer to becoming your best self. Have a good time! Enjoy them, enjoy being yourself, and enjoy your amazing existence.[161][162][163]

Self-care, self-compassion, and self-love may appear self-indulgent and indulgent. However, it is critical to your mental health and well-being. That doesn't mean you have to always put your needs before everyone else's. Having a healthy connection with oneself is, in fact, a selfless endeavor. Because how you treat others frequently mirrors how you treat yourself. If you're single, Valentine's Day might be difficult. From Cinderella to Bridget Jones, popular culture tells us that romantic love is the only way to genuine happiness. Finding 'The One is the ultimate goal — and if we're single, we've failed at life somehow. But this is a myth. Yes, a love connection may lead to contentment. However, it is not the only one. And singledom has increased dramatically in recent decades.

You may be single and content. You may be in a relationship while being miserable. What counts most is your relationship with yourself. This is because external validation can never satisfy your feeling of self-worth: it must come from within. Loving oneself sets the tone for your interactions with others. A lack of self-love may attract problematic relationships since it is more difficult to tolerate other people treating you poorly when you genuinely love yourself. Because if you're always seeking other factors to validate your sense of self-worth, you're bound to be disappointed. This confidence should instead come from the inside.

---

[161] "9 Types of Meditation: Which One Is Right for You?." 05 Nov. 2021, https://www.healthline.com/health/mental-health/types-of-meditation.
[162] "5-Minute Meditation You Can Do Anywhere - YouTube." https://www.youtube.com/watch?v=inpok4MKVLM.
[163] "How To Meditate - 6 Ways to Learn How to Meditate - Chopra." 11 Aug. 2019, https://chopra.com/articles/learn-to-meditate-in-6-easy-steps.

Having a positive relationship with oneself is essential for mental health. Being nice to oneself reduces anxiety and stress while developing self-esteem and resilience. Furthermore, suppose you don't cultivate a positive relationship with yourself. In that case, you may acquire negative habits such as people-pleasing and perfectionism – and you may be more prone to suffer abuse or maltreatment. "Love yourself!" we hear all the time. We are often told that loving ourselves is the most essential and useful thing we can do. But what we don't often hear, or comprehend, is how. What exactly is self-love? What does it mean to put it into practice? How do we get started?

Self-love means having a compassionate, kind, patient, tolerable, and curious relationship with yourself. It does not imply that you are so good to yourself that you never accept accountability or responsibility for your faults - "Oh, well, I love myself and think I'm fantastic so that it couldn't be my fault!" Giving oneself compassion and forgiveness when you make errors is part of self-love. It does not imply that you are arrogant or, worse, a narcissist: "I am superior to everyone else, and everyone should try to meet my wants." It is all about believing in yourself and trusting your objectives.

Because you can't provide healthy love to others unless you first love yourself, you may feel affection for others, yet you may be afraid to show it. You may love people and wish to relate to them, but you will find it difficult to receive healthy love if you do not first love yourself. In a good relationship, the exchange of love necessitates concrete self-love. Because an empty cup cannot be poured from, consider how much work it takes to show love and affection, be emotionally open, or be attentive. If you don't have reservoirs of self-love within you, your ability to offer love will suffer because self-love heals old scars and traumas. Many of us have had challenges that have affected our mental health, sense of self, attitude, and worldview. Traumas can leave us feeling as if we are less valuable than we were before the occurrence. Cultivating our feeling of self-love to originate from inside rather than from elsewhere assists us in moving past previous bad experiences.

Because having self-love allows you to establish better, healthier, more true objectives for yourself. How often have you established a goal for yourself based on negativity: disliking your physique, feeling helpless at work, or feeling like a "failure" at a pastime or passion? We want to nurture ourselves rather than "fix" ourselves with arbitrary expectations when we love ourselves. Now that we have a better grasp of our own beliefs and capabilities, we can make better decisions about our goals.

<-END->

References

1. "Good Vibes, Good Life: How Self-Love Is the Key to Unlocking Your ...." https://www.goodreads.com/book/show/42186465-good-vibes-good-life.

2. "Self-Love and What It Means - Brain & Behavior Research Foundation." 12 Feb. 2020, https://www.bbrfoundation.org/blog/self-love-and-what-it-means.

3. "What is Self-Love and Why Is It So Important? - Psych Central." 31 May. 2019, https://psychcentral.com/blog/imperfect/2019/05/what-is-self-love-and-why-is-it-so-important.

4. "Self Love: Definition, Tips, Examples, and Exercises." https://www.berkeleywellbeing.com/self-love.html.

5. "Self-love - Wikipedia." https://en.wikipedia.org/wiki/Self-love.

6. "What is Self-Love | The Importance of Self Love | How to Practice Self ...." https://www.growingself.com/what-is-self-love/.

7. "Self-love - Wikipedia." https://en.wikipedia.org/wiki/Self-love.

8. "Self-Love and What It Means - Brain & Behavior Research Foundation." 12 Feb. 2020, https://www.bbrfoundation.org/blog/self-love-and-what-it-means.

9. "What is Self-Love and Why Is It So Important? - Psych Central." 31 May. 2019,

https://psychcentral.com/blog/imperfect/2019/05/what-is-self-love-and-why-is-it-so-important.

10. "Self Love: Definition, Tips, Examples, and Exercises." https://www.berkeleywellbeing.com/self-love.html.

11. "Self-love - Wikipedia." https://en.wikipedia.org/wiki/Self-love.

12. "What is Self-Love | The Importance of Self Love | How to Practice Self ...." https://www.growingself.com/what-is-self-love/.

13. "Self-Love | Psychology Today." 12 Nov. 2019, https://www.psychologytoday.com/us/blog/the-upside-things/201911/self-love.

14. "8 Powerful Steps to Self-Love | Psychology Today." 29 Jun. 2017, https://www.psychologytoday.com/us/blog/the-mindful-self-express/201706/8-powerful-steps-self-love.

15. "41 Ways to Practice Self-Love and Be Good to Yourself." 10 Mar. 2022, https://www.lifehack.org/articles/communication/30-ways-practice-self-love-and-good-yourself.html.

16. "Just Love Yourself: 5 Must-Know Self-Love Techniques." 10 Jan. 2020, https://blog.mindvalley.com/self-love-techniques/.

17. "What is another word for self-aware? - WordHippo." https://www.wordhippo.com/what-is/another-word-for/self-aware.html.

18. "10 Simple Ways to Improve Your Self-Awareness [With Examples]." 04 Nov. 2021, https://nickwignall.com/self-awareness/.

19. "Self-awareness Definition & Meaning - Merriam-Webster." https://www.merriam-webster.com/dictionary/self-awareness.

20. "The importance of self-love and how to cultivate it." 23 Mar. 2018, https://www.medicalnewstoday.com/articles/321309.

21. "How to Be More Self Aware: 8 Tips to Boost Self-Awareness." 17 Oct. 2019, https://www.developgoodhabits.com/what-is-self-awareness/.

22. "About Self-Love: What is Self Love?." https://pathofselflove.org/about/about-self-love/.

23. "10 Tangible Ways To Practice Self-Love—Lists, Rituals & More." 13 Feb. 2020, https://www.mindbodygreen.com/0-12428/10-wonderful-ways-to-practice-selflove.html.

24. "Pentingnya Self-Love dan Cara Menerapkannya - Alodokter." https://www.alodokter.com/pentingnya-self-love-dan-cara-menerapkannya.

25. "What Is Self-Awareness and Why Is It Important? [+5 Ways to Increase It]." 24 Apr. 2022, https://positivepsychology.com/self-awareness-matters-how-you-can-be-more-self-aware/.

26. "Case Study: Becoming Self-Aware • Partnership for Public Service." https://ourpublicservice.org/public-service-leadership-institute/tools/case-study-becoming-self-aware/.

27. "Self-Awareness Test: How Self-Aware Are You? - My Question Life." 04 May. 2020, https://myquestionlife.com/self-awareness-test/.

28. "8 simple ways to practise self-love | Mental Health Foundation." 23 Oct. 2018,

https://www.mentalhealth.org.uk/blog/8-simple-ways-practise-self-love.

29. "How to Love Yourself: 6 Therapist-Backed Tips for Practicing Self-Love ...." 04 Mar. 2022, https://www.self.com/story/how-to-love-yourself.

30. "Increase Clients' Self-Love: 30 Exercises, Techniques and Worksheets." 29 May. 2022, https://positivepsychology.com/self-love-exercises-worksheets/.

31. "Self Love Quotes (3920 quotes) - Goodreads." https://www.goodreads.com/quotes/tag/self-love.

32. "7 Examples of Self-Awareness (and Why It's so Important)." 03 May. 2022, https://www.trackinghappiness.com/why-self-awareness-important/.

33. "15 signs you're more self-aware than you may think - Ideapod." 20 Oct. 2021, https://ideapod.com/signs-of-self-awareness/.

34. "15 signs you're more self-aware than you may think - Ideapod." 20 Oct. 2021, https://ideapod.com/signs-of-self-awareness/.

35. "Self-love Definition & Meaning - Merriam-Webster." https://www.merriam-webster.com/dictionary/self-love.

36. "13 Habits of Self-Love Every Woman Should Adopt - Healthline." 18 Sept. 2018, https://www.healthline.com/health/13-self-love-habits-every-woman-needs-to-have.

37. "Self Love – What it Actually Means: Misconceptions Shattered." 03 Mar. 2022, https://joannabel.com/self-love/.

38. "Self-Care - Active Minds." https://www.activeminds.org/about-mental-health/self-care/.

39. "5 Self-Care Practices for Every Area of Your Life - Verywell Mind." 23 May. 2022, https://www.verywellmind.com/self-care-strategies-overall-stress-reduction-3144729.

40. "Self-Care: 12 Ways to Take Better Care of Yourself." 28 Dec. 2018, https://www.psychologytoday.com/us/blog/click-here-happiness/201812/self-care-12-ways-take-better-care-yourself.

41. "What Is Self-Care and Why Is It Critical for Your Health?." 19 May. 2021, https://www.everydayhealth.com/self-care/.

42. "Self-Care: Definition and Examples - Verywell Health." 04 Jan. 2022, https://www.verywellhealth.com/self-care-definition-and-examples-5212781.

43. "What Self-Awareness Really Is (and How to Cultivate It)." 04 Jan. 2018, https://hbr.org/2018/01/what-self-awareness-really-is-and-how-to-cultivate-it.

44. "7 Tips for Improving Your Self-Awareness | Psych Central." 05 May. 2022, https://psychcentral.com/health/how-to-be-more-self-aware-and-why-its-important.

45. "What Is Self-Awareness, and How Do You Get It? | Psychology Today." 11 Mar. 2019, https://www.psychologytoday.com/us/blog/click-here-happiness/201903/what-is-self-awareness-and-how-do-you-get-it.

46. "Self Care 101 | Psychology Today." 27 May. 2018, https://www.psychologytoday.com/us/blog/skinny-revisited/201805/self-care-101.

47. "What is self-care? | Global Self-Care Federation." https://www.selfcarefederation.org/what-is-self-care.

48. "Self-care tips: The complete guide to taking care of yourself." https://www.tonyrobbins.com/mental-health/self-care-tips/.

49. "Self-aware - definition of self-aware by The Free Dictionary." https://www.thefreedictionary.com/self-aware.

50. "The True Meaning of Self-Awareness (& How to Tell If You're Actually ...." 11 May. 2018, https://blog.hubspot.com/marketing/self-awareness.

51. "Self-Awareness: Why It's Good for You and How to Develop It." 21 Apr. 2022, https://psychcentral.com/health/self-awareness.

52. "What is Self-Care? - Habits for Wellbeing." 07 Jun. 2014, https://www.habitsforwellbeing.com/what-is-self-care/.

53. "A guide to self-care - Life in Mind Australia." https://lifeinmind.org.au/research/self-care.

54. "What Is Self-Awareness? (And How To Increase Yours)." 09 Sept. 2021, https://www.indeed.com/career-advice/career-development/what-is-self-awareness.

55. "Self-awareness - Wikipedia." https://en.wikipedia.org/wiki/Self-awareness.

56. "What Is Self-Awareness, and Why Is It Important? - BetterUp." 21 Apr. 2021, https://www.betterup.com/blog/what-is-self-awareness.

57. "What Is Self-Care? - Healthline." 03 Sept. 2019, https://www.healthline.com/health-news/self-care-is-not-just-treating-yourself.

58. "What Is Self-Awareness and How Does It Develop?." 14 Jul. 2020, https://www.verywellmind.com/what-is-self-awareness-2795023.

59. "Self-aware Definition & Meaning - Merriam-Webster." https://www.merriam-webster.com/dictionary/self-aware.

60. "What Is Self-Care & Why Is Caring About Yourself Important?." https://thelawofattraction.com/self-care-tips/.

61. "30 Self-Care Habits for a Strong and Healthy Mind, Body and Spirit." https://www.lifehack.org/834747/self-care.

62. "What Is Self-Care? 30 Best Self Care Ideas, Activities and Apps." 02 Sept. 2021, https://parade.com/1039023/allisonscerbomusante/what-is-self-care/.

63. "Self-Care: What It Really Is and How to Do It Well." 27 Apr. 2020, https://nickwignall.com/self-care/.

64. "What is Self-Care? - ISF." https://isfglobal.org/what-is-self-care/.

65. "Self-Care Tips | Agency for Integrated Care - AIC." https://www.aic.sg/caregiving/self-care-tips.

66. "Self-care - Wikipedia." https://en.wikipedia.org/wiki/Self-care.

67. "Why is Self-Care Important? - SNHU." 14 Apr. 2020, https://www.snhu.edu/about-us/newsroom/health/what-is-self-care.

68. "Self Care." https://selfcare.time.com.my/auth/login.
69. "Self-Talk | Psychology Today." https://www.psychologytoday.com/us/basics/self-talk.
70. "Self-Talk: Why It Matters - Healthline." 12 Jul. 2016, https://www.healthline.com/health/mental-health/self-talk.
71. "Positive Self-Talk: Benefits and Techniques - Healthline." 17 Oct. 2018, https://www.healthline.com/health/positive-self-talk.
72. "What is Positive Self-Talk? (Incl. Examples)." 21 Sept. 2021, https://positivepsychology.com/positive-self-talk/.
73. "What Is Self-Talk - Think Affirmations." 05 Jan. 2021, https://thinkaffirmations.com/self-talk/.
74. "15 Ways to Practice Positive Self-Talk for Success - Lifehack." https://www.lifehack.org/504756/self-talk-determines-your-success-15-tips.
75. "Mindfulness & Meditation - Harvard University." https://www.harvard.edu/in-focus/mindfulness-meditation/.
76. "Meditation for Beginners: 20 Practical Tips for ... - zen habits." https://zenhabits.net/meditation-guide/.
77. "4 Common Types of Self-Talk - Mindful." 12 Sept. 2016, https://www.mindful.org/4-common-types-self-talk/.
78. "Positive thinking: Reduce stress by eliminating negative self-talk ...." 03 Feb. 2022, https://www.mayoclinic.org/healthy-lifestyle/stress-management/in-depth/positive-thinking/art-20043950.

79. "What is Meditation - Headspace." https://www.headspace.com/meditation-101/what-is-meditation.

80. "What Does Meditation Mean? Meditation Definition (And Why It Matters)." https://mindworks.org/blog/meditation-definition/.

81. "Beginners Guide to Meditation: Techniques & Tips to Learn to Sit [Video]." https://mindworks.org/blog/beginners-guide-meditation/.

82. "Change Your Self-Talk | Psychology Today." 05 Nov. 2019, https://www.psychologytoday.com/us/blog/loving-through-your-differences/201911/change-your-self-talk.

83. "Negative Self Talk: What It Is and Strategies To Stop It." https://mantracare.org/therapy/self-care/negative-self-talk/.

84. "Listening to self-talk for 15 minutes a day can change your life.." https://www.selftalkplus.com/.

85. "The Power of Positive Self Talk (and How You Can Use It)." 09 Jun. 2021, https://www.betterup.com/blog/self-talk.

86. "How to Do Positive Self-Talk - The Wellness Society | Self-Help ...." https://thewellnesssociety.org/positive-self-talk/.

87. "Self-Talk Plus+ on the App Store." 03 May. 2021, https://apps.apple.com/us/app/self-talk-plus/id1562158353.

88. "How To Meditate - Meditation 101: Meditation Techniques & Benefits ...." https://www.gaiam.com/blogs/discover/meditation-101-techniques-benefits-and-a-beginner-s-how-to.

89. "Sahaja Yoga Meditation." https://www.singaporemeditation.org/.

90. "Self-talk - what is it and why is it important? | healthdirect." https://www.healthdirect.gov.au/self-talk.

91. "Positive self-talk: Benefits, examples, and tips." 18 Mar. 2022, https://www.medicalnewstoday.com/articles/positive-self-talk.

92. "SELF-TALK - Winona State University." 29 Nov. 2016, https://www.winona.edu/resilience/Media/Self-Talk-Worksheet.pdf.

93. "Self-Talk Scripts: List Of Positive Affirmations [500+]." 31 Jan. 2019, https://mindbodypal.com/self-talk-scripts/.

94. "Parker Jack – Self Talk Lyrics | Genius Lyrics." 11 Mar. 2022, https://genius.com/Parker-jack-self-talk-lyrics.

95. "Self-Talk - InsideEWU." https://inside.ewu.edu/calelearning/psychological-skills/self-talk/.

96. "Self-Compassion." https://self-compassion.org/.

97. "How to Practice Self-Compassion: 8 Techniques and Tips." 26 Oct. 2021, https://positivepsychology.com/how-to-practice-self-compassion/.

98. "Self–Compassion - GoodTherapy." 17 Jun. 2019, https://www.goodtherapy.org/learn-about-therapy/issues/self-compassion.

99. "What is self-compassion? - Johns Hopkins University Student Well-Being." 04 Dec. 2020, https://wellbeing.jhu.edu/what-is-self-compassion/.

100. "Self-Compassion: Definition, Examples, and Exercises." https://www.berkeleywellbeing.com/self-compassion.html.

101. "Self-Compassion - The Center for Compassion and Altruism Research and ...." http://ccare.stanford.edu/research/wiki/compassion-definitions/self-compassion/.

102. "4 ways to boost your self-compassion - Harvard Health." 12 Feb. 2021, https://www.health.harvard.edu/mental-health/4-ways-to-boost-your-self-compassion.

103. "How to Practice Self-Compassion (Article) | Therapist Aid." https://www.therapistaid.com/therapy-article/how-to-practice-self-compassion.

104. "9 Powerful Self-Compassion Exercises & Worksheets (+ PDF)." 13 Jan. 2020, https://positivepsychology.com/self-compassion-exercises-worksheets/.

105. "Self-Compassion Quiz | Greater Good." https://greatergood.berkeley.edu/quizzes/take_quiz/self_compassion.

106. "Self-Compassion - Emotional Affair." https://www.emotionalaffair.org/wp-content/uploads/2012/10/Self-compassion.pdf.

107. "Developing Self-Compassion for Beginners - The Wellness Society | Self ...." https://thewellnesssociety.org/self-compassion/.

108. "Mindful Self-Compassion | Centers for Integrative Health." https://cih.ucsd.edu/mindfulness/mindful-self-compassion.

109. "The Five Myths of Self-Compassion - Greater Good." 30 Sept. 2015, https://greatergood.berkeley.edu/article/item/the_five_myths_of_self_compassion.

110. "How to practice self compassion and tame your inner critic." 18 Jun. 2021, https://www.betterup.com/blog/self-compassion.

111. "The power of self-compassion - Harvard Health." 02 Feb. 2022, https://www.health.harvard.edu/healthbeat/the-power-of-self-compassion.

112. "Self-compassion - Wikipedia." https://en.wikipedia.org/wiki/Self-compassion.

113. "What is Self-Compassion? Components, Myths, and Strategies." 27 Jun. 2012, https://psychcentral.com/blog/5-strategies-for-self-compassion.

114. "Self-Compassion | Trauma Recovery." https://trauma-recovery.ca/recovery/self-compassion/.

115. "Self-Compassion - an overview | ScienceDirect Topics." https://www.sciencedirect.com/topics/psychology/self-compassion.

116. "What is Self-Confidence? - University of South Florida." https://www.usf.edu/student-affairs/counseling-center/top-concerns/what-is-self-confidence.aspx.

117. "What Is Self-Confidence? | HealthyPlace." 04 Jun. 2022, https://www.healthyplace.com/self-help/self-confidence/what-is-self-confidence.

118. "What is Self-Confidence? + 9 Ways to Increase It [2019 Update]." 22 Dec. 2020, https://positivepsychology.com/self-confidence/.

119. "How to Build Self-Confidence - Stress Management from Mind Tools." https://www.mindtools.com/selfconf.html.

120. "How to Boost Your Self-Confidence - Verywell Mind." 14 Feb. 2022, https://www.verywellmind.com/how-to-boost-your-self-confidence-4163098.

121. "How To Build Self-Confidence in 7 Steps | Indeed.com." 13 Aug. 2021, https://www.indeed.com/career-advice/career-development/how-to-build-self-confidence.

122. "What is Self Confidence and Why is it Important?." 25 Apr. 2019, https://cognitiveheights.com/what-is-self-confidence-and-why-is-it-important/.

123. "12 Tips For Building Self-Confidence and Self-Belief (+PDF Worksheets)." 16 Jan. 2022, https://positivepsychology.com/self-confidence-self-belief/.

124. "Why Self-Confidence Is More Important Than You Think." 20 Sept. 2018, https://www.psychologytoday.com/us/blog/shyness-is-nice/201809/why-self-confidence-is-more-important-you-think.

125. "Self-confidence Definition & Meaning - Merriam-Webster." https://www.merriam-webster.com/dictionary/self-confidence.

126. "65 Synonyms & Antonyms of SELF-CONFIDENCE - Merriam-Webster." https://www.merriam-webster.com/thesaurus/self-confidence.

127. "self confidence Crossword Clue | Wordplays.com." https://www.wordplays.com/crossword-solver/self-confidence.

128. "Self-Confidence in the Workplace: Why It's Important and How To Improve ...." 10 Mar. 2021, https://www.indeed.com/career-advice/career-development/self-confidence.

129. "How to Build Self Confidence (with Pictures) - wikiHow." 16 Apr. 2022, https://www.wikihow.com/Build-Self-Confidence.

130. "14 Methods to Dramatically Increase Your Self-Confidence." https://www.cornerstone.edu/blog-post/14-methods-to-dramatically-increase-your-self-confidence/.

131. "How to Build Self-Confidence - Verywell Health." 15 Nov. 2021, https://www.verywellhealth.com/how-to-build-self-confidence-5209231.

132. "Building Confidence and Self-Esteem | Psychology Today." 30 May. 2012, https://www.psychologytoday.com/us/blog/hide-and-seek/201205/building-confidence-and-self-esteem.

133. "Self Confidence | Definition, Importance for Career, Ways to Improve." https://www.cleverism.com/skills-and-tools/self-confidence/.

134. "Building Your Self-Confidence - Mind Tools." https://www.mindtools.com/downloads/lbr5283hs/BuildingYourSelfConfidence.pdf.

135. "Self-Confidence: Definition, Affirmations, and Tips for Gaining ...." https://www.berkeleywellbeing.com/self-confidence.html.

136. "What is Mindfulness? - Mindful." 08 Jul. 2020, https://www.mindful.org/what-is-mindfulness/.

137. "Mindfulness journal." https://binaries.templates.cdn.office.net/support/templates/en-us/tf34169450_wac.docx.

138. "Mindfulness | Psychology Today." https://www.psychologytoday.com/us/basics/mindfulness.

139. "Mindfulness Definition | What Is Mindfulness - Greater Good." https://greatergood.berkeley.edu/topic/mindfulness/definition.

140. "Mindfulness exercises - Mayo Clinic." 15 Sept. 2020, https://www.mayoclinic.org/healthy-lifestyle/consumer-health/in-depth/mindfulness-exercises/art-20046356.

141. "Mindfulness - Wikipedia." https://en.wikipedia.org/wiki/Mindfulness.

142. "What Is Mindfulness? | Taking Charge of Your Health & Wellbeing." https://www.takingcharge.csh.umn.edu/what-mindfulness.

143. "How to Practice Mindfulness - Mindful." 12 Dec. 2018, https://www.mindful.org/how-to-practice-mindfulness/.

144. "How to Practice Mindfulness: 11 Practical Steps and Tips." 06 Oct. 2021, https://positivepsychology.com/how-to-practice-mindfulness/.

145. "The Benefits of Mindfulness - Verywell Mind." 15 Oct. 2021, https://www.verywellmind.com/the-benefits-of-mindfulness-5205137.

146. "Benefits of Mindfulness: Mindful Living Can Change Your Life." https://mindfulness.com/mindful-living/benefits.
147. "Mindfulness & Meditation - Harvard University." https://www.harvard.edu/in-focus/mindfulness-meditation/.
148. "12 Fun Mindfulness Exercises - The American Institute of Stress." 10 Feb. 2021, https://www.stress.org/12-fun-mindfulness-exercises.
149. "6 Mindfulness Exercises You Can Try Today." 27 Oct. 2017, https://www.pocketmindfulness.com/6-mindfulness-exercises-you-can-try-today/.
150. "22 Mindfulness Exercises & Activities For Adults (+ PDF)." 06 Feb. 2022, https://positivepsychology.com/mindfulness-exercises-techniques-activities/.
151. "Mindfulness.com - #1 App for Mindful Living, Meditation, & Breathwork ...." https://mindfulness.com/.
152. "Reduce Stress Through Mindfulness - Whole Health." https://www.va.gov/WHOLEHEALTH/features/Reduce_Stress_Through_Mindfulness.asp.
153. "What is mindfulness? - Mind." https://www.mind.org.uk/information-support/drugs-and-treatments/mindfulness/about-mindfulness/.
154. "Mindfulness: How It Helps Your Health - WebMD." https://www.webmd.com/balance/guide/what-is-mindfulness.
155. "Mindfulness for Beginners | Psychology Today." 12 Jul. 2017, https://www.psychologytoday.com/us/blog/how-be-yourself/201707/mindfulness-beginners.

156. "Mindfulness - Mental health and wellbeing | healthdirect." https://www.healthdirect.gov.au/mindfulness.

157. "Meditation - Mayo Clinic." 05 May. 2022, https://www.mayoclinic.org/tests-procedures/meditation/about/pac-20385120.

158. "How to Meditate - Mindful." https://www.mindful.org/how-to-meditate/.

159. "Meditation | Psychology Today." https://www.psychologytoday.com/us/basics/meditation.

160. "Meditation - Wikipedia." https://en.wikipedia.org/wiki/Meditation.

161. "Meditation: In Depth | NCCIH." https://www.nccih.nih.gov/health/meditation-in-depth.

162. "Meditation: Take a stress-reduction break wherever you are - Mayo Clinic." 29 Apr. 2022, https://www.mayoclinic.org/tests-procedures/meditation/in-depth/meditation/art-20045858.

163. "9 Types of Meditation: Which One Is Right for You?." 05 Nov. 2021, https://www.healthline.com/health/mental-health/types-of-meditation.

164. "5-Minute Meditation You Can Do Anywhere - YouTube." https://www.youtube.com/watch?v=inpok4MKVLM.

165. "How To Meditate - 6 Ways To Learn How To Meditate - Chopra." 11 Aug. 2019, https://chopra.com/articles/learn-to-meditate-in-6-easy-steps.

www.ingramcontent.com/pod-product-compliance
Lightning Source LLC
Chambersburg PA
CBHW020310010526
44107CB00001B/55